Recording Vocals with Dave Pensado

PENSADO'S PLACE
Pensado's STRIVE
STRIVE SERIES

Recording Vocals with Dave Pensado

DAVE PENSADO
Adaptation by BILL GIBSON

BASED ON THE AUDIOVISUAL COURSE
RECORDING VOCALS WITH DAVE PENSADO
AVAILABLE ON GROOVE3.COM

Hal Leonard Books
An Imprint of Hal Leonard LLC

Published in 2018 by Hal Leonard Books
An Imprint of Hal Leonard LLC
7777 West Bluemound Road
Milwaukee, WI 53213

Trade Book Division Editorial Offices
33 Plymouth St., Montclair, NJ 07042

CREDITS

Grateful acknowledgment is made to the following individuals and companies whose product images and photographs may appear in this book:

AEA Ribbon Mics & Preamps; AMS/Neve; Audio-Technica; Avalon Industries, Inc.; Avid; Brauner Microphones; Celemony; Stanley Coutant; David Hill Designs; eiosis; Electro-Voice; FabFilter Software Instruments; Georg Neumann GmbH; GML, LLC; Harman; IK Multimedia; Klangehelm Audio Plugins; Kush Audio; Mathew Lane; Latch Lake Music Products; Locomotive Audio; Maag Audio; Manley Laboratories; Martinsound; Massey Plug-Ins, Inc.; McDSP; Millennia Music & Media Systems; Royer Labs Microphones; Sennheiser; Shure; Sony Music Entertainment; Summit Audio; Synchro Arts; RCA; TELEFUNKEN Elektroakustik; Tube-Tech; Universal Audio; Waves

Printed in the United States of America
Book design by Kristina Rolander

Library of Congress Cataloging-in-Publication Data

Names: Pensado, Dave, author. | Gibson, Bill (William A.)
Title: Recording vocals with Dave Pensado / Dave Pensado; adaptation by Bill Gibson.
Description: Montclair, NJ : Hal Leonard Books, 2018. | Series: Pensado's strive education series | Includes index. | "Based on the audiovisual course Recording Vocals with Dave Pensado available on Groove3.com."
Identifiers: LCCN 2017057203 | ISBN 9781495092428 (pbk.)
Subjects: LCSH: Sound recordings--Production and direction. | Popular music--Production and direction.
Classification: LCC ML3790 .P417 2018 | DDC 782.049--dc23
LC record available at https://lccn.loc.gov/2017057203

www.halleonardbooks.com

Contents

Introduction

Recording Vocals with Dave Pensado shares many of the insider tricks and secrets that I've discovered throughout my career in the recording business. I've been fortunate enough to work with some of the brightest stars in the music world, from Beyoncé to the Black Eyed Peas and from Michael Jackson to Macy Gray. And throughout my time in the studio, I've found ways to get the most out of a vocalist by making sure they're physically, emotionally, and musically comfortable.

As you work through this book, I'll show you how a top-level session works, all the way from getting ready for the artist's arrival at the studio through tracking, tightening, tuning, and mixing world-class vocals. If you think back to when you first discovered music, it's very likely that what you fell in love with was the vocal performance and the emotional energy that it added to the music. I do my best to always keep it in the front of my mind when I'm recording and mixing a record. My approach to vocals might be a little different than what you're accustomed to. I've developed an unconventional approach to applying plug-ins that I think makes the best use out of each processing tool that I use. In this book, you're very likely to discover some very important thoughts and techniques that will definitely help you record and mix better vocals.

Recording Vocals with Dave Pensado

1

How Microphones Work

Let's start by diving into how microphones work, both from a creative and a technical standpoint. There are all kinds of microphones but for our purposes in recording vocals, we'll focus on three types: dynamic, condenser, and ribbon.

Fundamentally, microphone technology hasn't changed a lot over the years. However, with advances in manufacturing techniques and a constant push from microphone manufacturers to develop better mics, there have been quite a few improvements in specifications, consistency, and reliability. There are several amazing mics available to everyone today.

DYNAMIC MICROPHONES

Dynamic microphones are the bargain of the microphone world. They are durable, able to withstand loud sounds without overdriving, and they sound great on a lot of instruments and vocals.

A dynamic microphone is a fairly simple device. It works like a speaker but in reverse. With a speaker, the powered signal from a power amp varies the polarity of the speaker magnet. That change in magnetic polarity moves the voice coil that's suspended around the magnet up and down in direct correlation to the variations in north/south polarity. The voice coil is attached to the speaker cone. As the changes in magnetism move the voice coil, the cone is moved. It's the movement of the cone that causes variation in air pressure, which is what we perceive as sound.

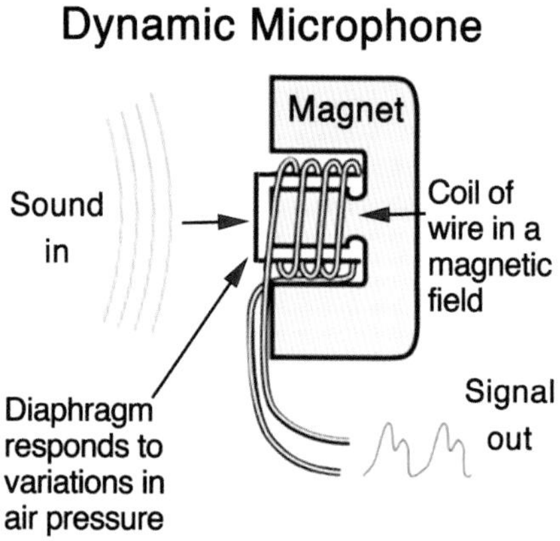

The dynamic microphone capsule

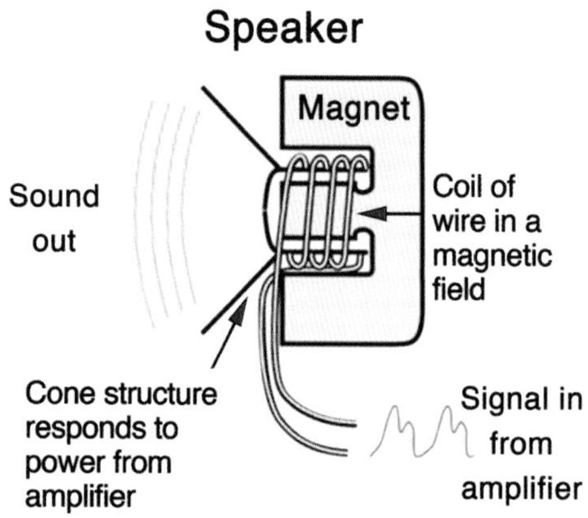

The speaker, voice coil, and speaker cone

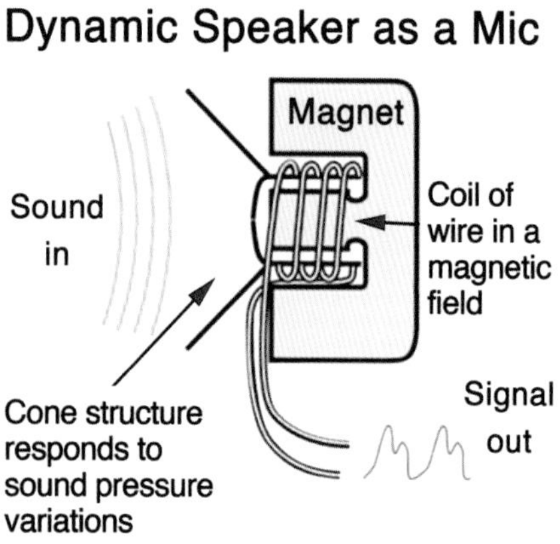

Using a speaker as a microphone

Conversely, a dynamic mic diaphragm—typically and very thin round plastic wafer—is sympathetically vibrated by sound waves in the air, which move the attached coil of thinly wound copper wire around a magnet. As the copper coil moves up and down, the flow of electrons in the magnet vary between north and south in direct correlation to the peaks and dips in the source waveform. The coil movement around the magnet causes a continuously changing polarity in the magnet, which is the origin of the electrical signal that's sent to the mixer or recorder.

But if we wire the positive and negative speaker terminals to pins 2 and 3 of an XLR connector, we can plug that XLR connector into a mixer input and the speaker will become a microphone that focuses on low frequencies. When recording drums, we frequently use the woofer from a Yamaha NS10 in front of the kick drum as a microphone for low frequencies.

Shure SM7B

The Shure SM7B is a dynamic mic and it's one of the great vocal mics of all time. It's a very affordable microphone. I've seen them used for around $300 and I've seen them new below $500. Bruce Swedien used an SM7—the original version of the SM7B—to record Michael Jackson on *Thriller.* That says a lot about the sound of this mic! If it's good enough for Michael....

The Shure SM7B

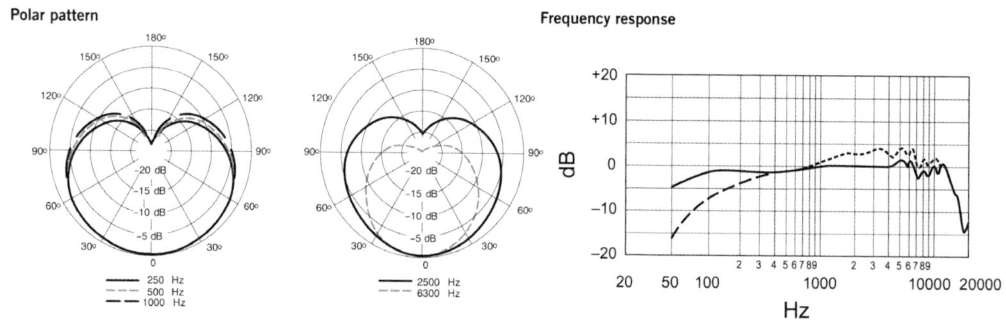

Frequency response graph with polar pattern

The SM7B comes with a bass roll-off, a mid-range enhancement button, and a pop filter. It has a cardioid polar pattern and frequency response range from 50–20,000 Hz. What a bargain!

Shure SM57 and SM58

In the same family with the Shure SM7B are the Shure SM57 and SM58. The 57 and 58 are nearly identical microphones. They use the same capsule but their physical housings are just a little different so their specifications are not exactly the same. The SM58 has a pop filter inside the ball-shaped, screw-on head. The SM57 has a more streamlined head that covers the diaphragm and it doesn't have a pop filter. Both the 57 and 58 exhibit cardioid polar patterns. The SM57 has a frequency response range from 40–15,000 Hz and the SM58's response range is from 50–15,000 Hz.

The Shure SM57

The Shure SM58

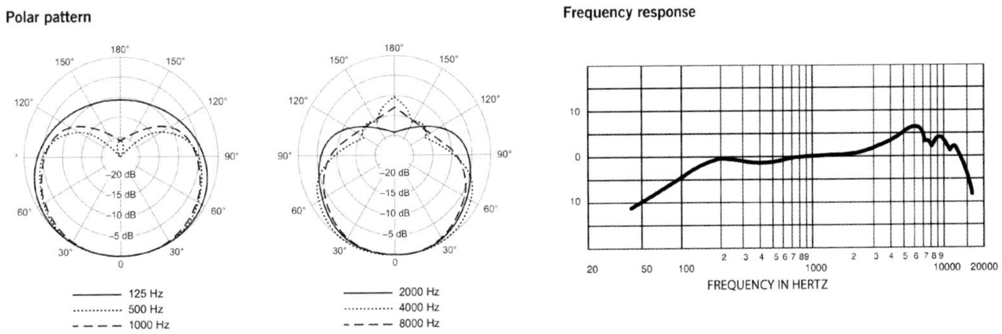

SM57 frequency response graph with polar pattern

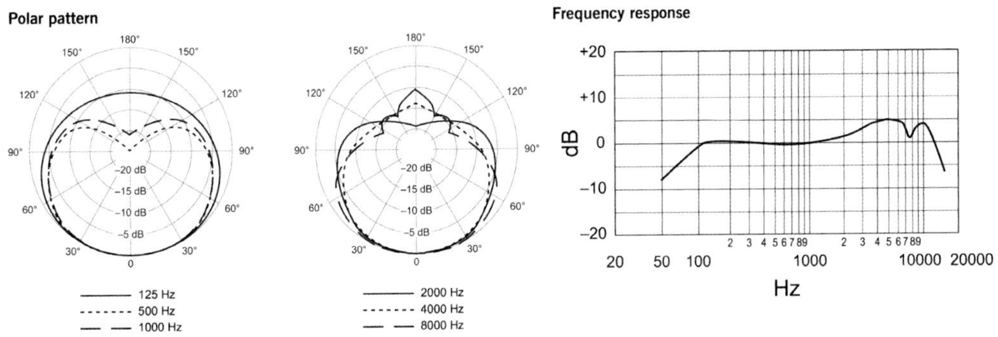

SM58 frequency response graph with polar pattern

Because of its pop filter, durability, cardioid polar pattern, reasonable price, and the fact that its frequency response highlights vocal intelligibility and clarity, the SM58 is the most commonly used mic for vocals and instruments in a live setting. It sounds full and clean at close distances on vocals and instruments and its inherent design helps minimize feedback.

Sennheiser MD 441

Another dynamic microphone I like an awful lot is the Sennheiser MD 441. It's that long, slender microphone you see Stevie Nicks using from time to time. It has a very useful five-position bass roll-off that adjusts the mic so it can sound good across a wider range of distances from the source. "Proximity effect" refers to the increase in bass response that happens naturally as the distance between the microphone and the source decreases. With the five-position bass roll-off, an engineer can fine-tune the impact of the proximity effect on the vocal sound by changing the amount of low-frequency roll-off. Starting in the first position (flat), each successive position increases the amount of roll-off and raises the cut-off frequency. The MD 441 also includes a high-frequency boost switch for better clarity on vocals and instruments.

It's important to be aware of the proximity effect. Just by moving the artist closer to the microphone or farther away, you can help shape the recorded vocal sound. Simply moving closer to the mic often helps a hip-hop artist or a rocker fill out their tone in the low end so their sound is more powerful. When vocalists sing loudly, they can easily decrease the bass in their sound by just moving a few inches away from the mic. The engineer and artist can work together, using the benefits of the proximity effect along with a variable low-frequency filter like the five-position switch on the Sennheiser 441 to shape a sound that's as intimate as the music calls for, while still having a very well-balanced sound.

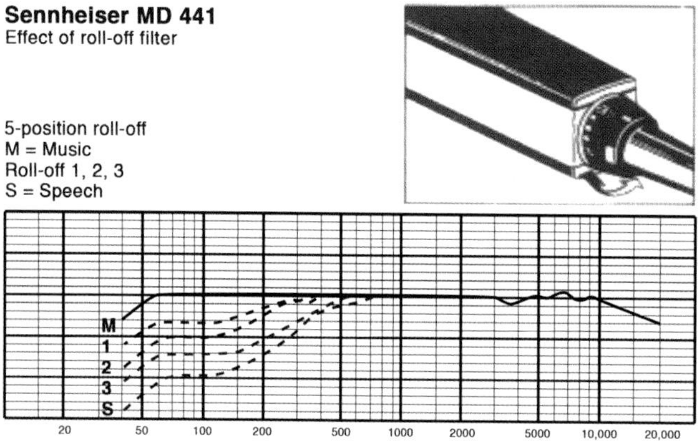

Sennheiser MD 441 frequency response graph with all five roll-off positions

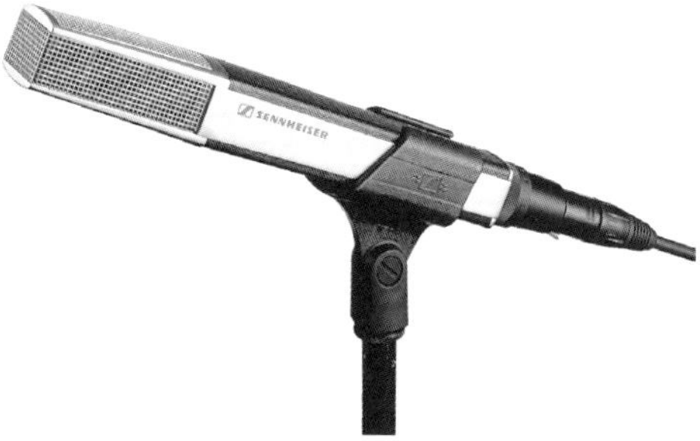

Sennheiser MD 441

CONDENSER MICROPHONES

The condenser capsule is a little more complicated than a dynamic mic. It's a big capacitor (a device that stores an electrical charge) with voltage interacting between two conductive plates: one solid plate and one piece of flexible Mylar that is thinly coated with a conductive alloy. A sound wave sympathetically vibrates the flexible plate, causing the electrical charge that has developed between the two plates to change in direct correlation with the crests and troughs in the audio wave. Comparing the dynamic capsule, which vibrates a membrane connected to a copper coil of wire around a magnet, with the condenser capsule, which simply vibrates a thin piece of plastic that has been lightly coated with a conductive material to vary electrically charged air, it's easy to see why the condenser would more accurately follow the waveform. Because of their inherent design, condenser mics are much better than dynamic mics at faithfully capturing transients and fine detail in the sound wave.

Condenser microphones tend to be more expensive than the other mic types. They require what is called "phantom power" to operate. Phantom power is typically a 48V DC current—the EIC phantom power standard also specifies 12- and 24-volt phantom power. It serves a couple of very important needs:

1. Phantom power supplies the polarizing voltage to the plates in the condenser capsule.
2. The signal that is generated by the condenser capsule is very weak and needs to be boosted up to mic level, which involves an amplifier circuit in the mic body (sometimes the amplifier is in an external box). Phantom power provides the power to run this amplifier.

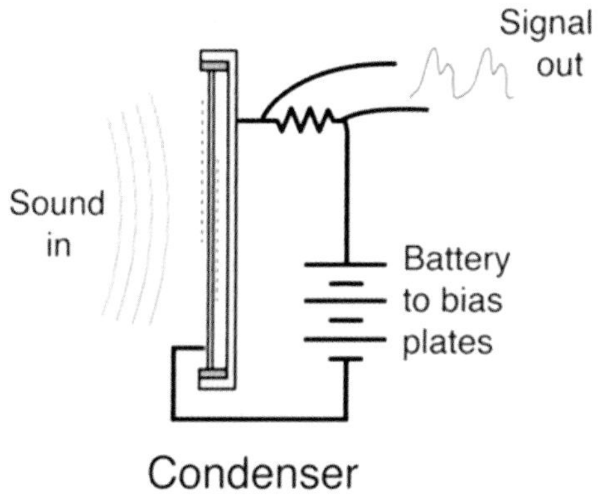

A simple illustration of the condenser capsule

A lot of condenser mics have multiple polar patterns. Many mics provide omnidirectional, bidirectional, and cardioid patterns. Some microphones even add variations of the cardioid polar response, such as hypercardioid, supercardioid, and subcardioid.

An omnidirectional condenser microphone provides a very true sound! But, you've got to be in a great-sounding room for omnidirectional mics to be effective. Unlike cardioid microphones, which sound thinner when you move even a little off-axis, omnidirectional mics sound the same from any angle. They tend to work great for vocalists who move around lot. That's not so true when using a dynamic cardioid microphone. A lot of times when I use a dynamic mic on a singer—these almost always exhibit a cardioid polar pattern—I let the singer hand-hold it. That way the vocalist can move around more and the mic can move too.

When it comes to recording vocals, the microphones that everyone talks about are the Telefunken 251s, the Neumann U 47s, the Sony C-800G, Neumann U 87, the Manley Labs Reference Cardioid Microphone, and there are more.

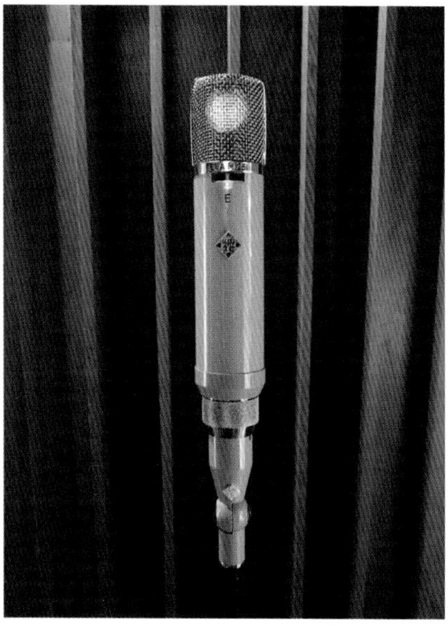

Telefunken ELAM 251

Early Neumann U 47
(FROM GEORG NEUMANN GMBH)

Sony C-800G

Neumann U 87
(FROM GEORG NEUMANN GMBH)

Manley Labs Reference Cardioid Microphone

RIBBON MICROPHONES

The last category is the ribbon microphone. It is like the dynamic mic because it involves metal moving in a magnetic field. A dynamic mic uses the motion of a copper coil surrounding a magnet as the source of its signal; however, a ribbon mic uses a thin metal ribbon (vibrated by sound waves) surrounded by a magnet as the source of its signal.

Classic ribbon mics needed a large magnet and a long ribbon to get a signal that was strong enough to feed the console. The weight of the mic and the thin ribbon made the ribbon very susceptible to breakage—it was fragile. Modern ribbon mics are pretty tough; though between dynamic, condenser, and ribbon mics, ribbon mics are still the most fragile. Vocals recorded on a ribbon mic sound a little dark for my taste but a lot of people like that sound, so experiment and see if the sound works for your recordings.

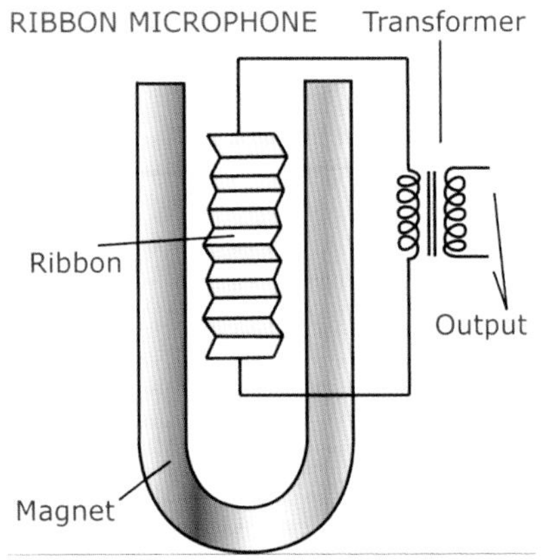

The ribbon microphone capsule

Royer and AEA make some excellent ribbon microphones. AEA makes a microphone called an N22 that requires phantom power. It has great frequency response. I love that microphone. I use it often. Even though the AEA N22 requires phantom power, most ribbon mics specifically do not use phantom power. Always turn the phantom power off on a ribbon microphone unless you know for sure that it needs it. Applying phantom power can blow the ribbon in the same way applying too much electricity blows a fuse.

Royer R-121

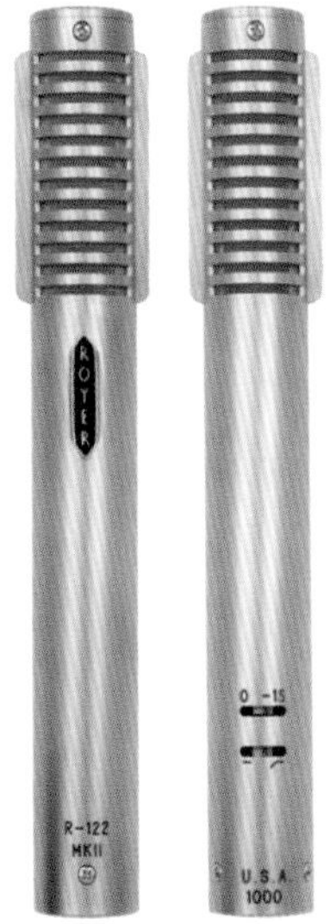

Royer R-122

AEA N22

MATCHING IMPEDANCE

Impedance is the measure of the resistance to the flow of current, measured in ohms and symbolized by the Omega sign (Ω). It is crucial that the input and output impedances work together to facilitate the best possible sound from the microphone. They don't have to match exactly but they need to work well together. If a low-impedance input receives a signal from a high-impedance device that expects to see a high-impedance input, there will be too little resistance to the signal and the input will probably distort, even with the input level turned way down. Conversely, if a high-impedance input receives a signal from a low-impedance device, there will be too much resistance to the signal and therefore, even when the input level is turned way up, there will probably be too little level—the sound at that input will be weak and noisy.

It is crucial that impedances are matched, low with low, and high with high, at each stage of the signal path: mic to preamp, preamp to console line input, console line output to the recorder/interface line input, and so on. Some microphone preamps provide an input impedance switch that sets the input impedance to exactly match the microphone's output impedance. With typical low-impedance microphones ranging from 150–1,000 ohms, setting the input impedance at 150 ohms to match the output impedance of the 150-ohm microphone optimizes the sound of the mic; setting the input impedance at 600 ohms to match the output impedance of 600-ohm microphone optimizes the sound of the mic; and so on.

When there is an impedance mismatch between a condenser microphone and the mixer or preamp input, it is likely to manifest itself as a rolled-off high-end or there might be some other unwanted coloration of the sound. A lot of people don't understand this but the signal that is produced by the condenser capsule is very weak. In fact, the capsule signal needs an amplifying circuit to achieve enough strength to be called "mic level." Most condenser mics use a solid-state amplifier built into the mic body to boost the capsule-level signal to a mic-level signal. With a tube microphone, like a Neumann U 47 or Telefunken ELAM 251, a tube amplifier is used to attain proper level.

SHAPING A POLAR PATTERN

To create various polar patterns within one microphone, mic designers discovered that when they super-imposed a figure-eight, bidirectional microphone on top of an omnidirectional microphone, the result was a different pattern than either the omnidirectional or bidirectional pattern—it was cardioid! It makes sense, really. If you consider that an omni mic is one 360-degree positive polarity mic that hears equally all the way around the mic, and if you consider that a bidirectional mic has a positive-polarity lobe on one side of the mic and a negative-polarity lobe on the other, it makes sense that combining the two would result in the signals that sum on the positive side of the bidirectional mic and cancel on the negative side of the bidirectional mic.

The result of combining the two signals to one input would be a mic with increased sensitivity on one side of the mic and decreased sensitivity on the other side of the mic. If the ratio of the two bidirectional lobes is altered, various types of cardioid patterns can be created. It is condenser microphones that use this concept to create a range of polar patterns. Since condenser mic capsules use electrical voltage to charge the moveable plate, storing electricity between the solid and moveable plates, it didn't take long for mic designers to figure out they could put another moveable plate on the other side of the solid pate, opening up all sorts of options for combining voltages. They could easily create polar patterns ranging from omnidirectional to bidirectional to cardioid, hypercardioid, supercardioid, and all the way to super long and narrow shotgun patterns.

It's kind of neat that you can have just one microphone and flip some switches and get all these different patterns. That's very useful. A cardioid pattern is particularly useful when you want to record the sound source without too much of a contribution from a bad-sounding room. If you're recording in a great-sounding room, you have the option to use an omnidirectional mic to capture some of that sound to enhance your recording.

The figure-eight, bidirectional pattern by itself is usually found in a ribbon microphone but it is also typically one of the selectable patterns on a multi-pattern condenser mic. Bidirectional mics have very good side rejection. Since one side of the bidirectional mic has a positive polarity and the other side has a negative polarity, any sound source that is 90 or 270 degrees off-axis is heard equally by the front (positive) and back (negative). So the output of the mic almost totally cancels sound directly from the sides of the capsule.

Once you start to see how these microphones work, it opens up your creativity and you can imagine where each of the mic types might work well. Obviously, a cardioid mic works well for live vocal-miking situations because it focuses on the vocalist and minimizes the leakage from the rest of the band and ambient noises. An omnidirectional mic wouldn't be a good choice on a vocalist in a live situation because, other than the fact that the vocalist is the closest thing to the mic, the mic isn't any more focused on the vocal than it is on the rest of the band, crowd noise, or sound system. Omni mics are the most prone to feedback, which is what happens when the mic hears the sound system and feeds that back into the sound system, then hears that again and forms a loop that manifests as a loud annoying squeal through the speakers.

2

How to Set Up Microphones

Setting up microphones might sound simple but there's a lot to it. I want to share some things with you that might enhance your recordings and get you a little money on the side too.

WINDSCREENS

Windscreens, also called "pop filters," are almost always made from foam rubber, nylon material (like women's pantyhose), or some synthetic material that emulates either of these.

The material needs to be light and porous enough to be sonically transparent but dense enough to diffuse the air generated by the pronunciation of strong sibilant sounds and plosives—hard consonants, like "P" and "B." Basically, we need to keep too much air from hitting the capsule. With no windscreen, it is very likely that your vocal recordings will contain excessive sibilant sounds and plosive problems, also called "P-pops," from the strong blasts of air at the beginning of words such as "potato" and "boomerang." We can fix a lot of these problems in the digital domain but it's much more time- and cost-efficient (and it sounds better) when we do what we can to get it right at the source.

This is Erik Reicher's room at Echo Bar Recording Studios in North Hollywood after a session he just had with Rasan Patterson.

Erik likes to keep the windscreen about a fist away from the microphone. Let the vocalist test the microphone from different distances until you find the optimum sound. Position the windscreen so it keeps the singer at that perfect position.

Nylon hoop windscreen

Foam windscreen

When I'm testing out a windscreen, I like to blow into the front of it while holding my hand behind it to feel how much air is being diffused. If there's a substantial reduction in the amount of air behind the windscreen, I know it will probably do a good job protecting the microphone capsule. If the windscreen lets too much air through, it probably won't do a good job. On the other hand, if you can't feel any air blowing through the windscreen, it's probably not the right windscreen either, because it might not be acoustically transparent. Before you purchase a windscreen, check it out and make sure it's working the way you want it to.

When I was first starting out, I couldn't afford a windscreen, no matter how inexpensive it was. So I would take an embroidery hoop and stretch some pantyhose over the opening. It worked great. It was perfect!

SHOCK MOUNTS AND STUDIO BOOM STANDS

Condenser mics—especially large-diaphragm studio condensers mics—are extremely sensitive to vibrations and rumbling that transmit up though the mic base and stand. And studio condenser mics don't tend to have built-in structural designs that guard against these vibrations combining with the vocal at the mic capsule. These vibrations travelling up through the mic stand and combining with the vocal take will almost always ruin the performance. It never happens during a bad take. It always happens during the take that's going to make you a rich and famous engineer and fill your bank account with tons of money. I promise you, that's the way it always happens. A shock mount that suspends the mic so it isn't touching the stand is the answer—shock mounts are critical components of the vocal-miking toolkit.

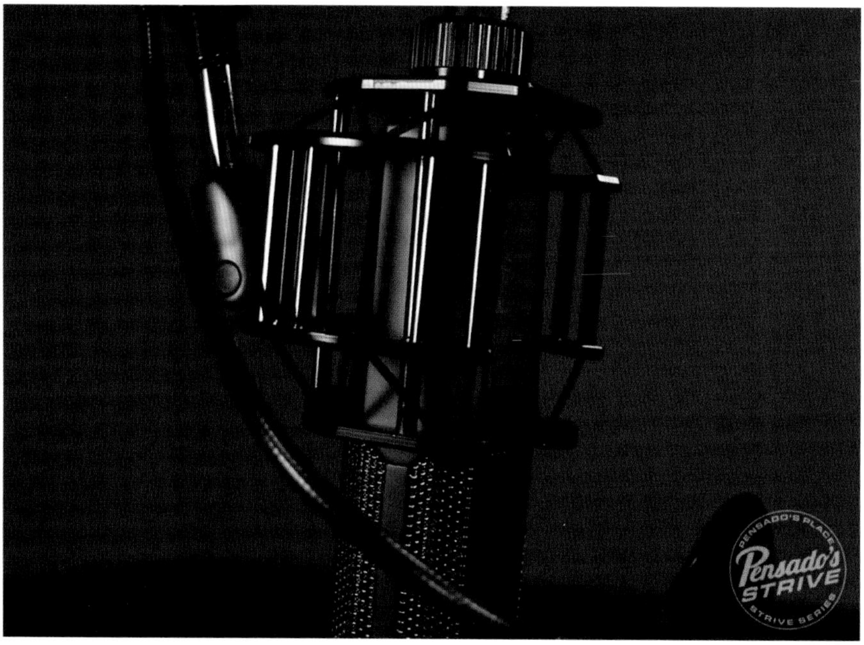

A typical shock mount consists of a metal frame that suspends around the body of the microphone and a sleeve that holds the mic body. Rubber or elastic bands connect to a series of hooks on the frame and sleeve in a way the suspends the microphone in the middle of the frame, effectively isolating the mic from any vibrations or rumbling.

It is important to make sure all shock mounts are maintained well and the bands are in good shape. If the mic stand base is solid enough, it's a good idea to put something like a thin foam pad under the mic stand base to reduce transmission from the floor. It is also quite standard when using a large studio boom stand to hold a bulky and expensive large-diaphragm condenser microphone to place sand bags on the stand base.

This Latch Lake micKing® Series studio boom is an excellent mic stand. It has a lot of great features.

If you take a close look at this boom stand, you'll see the mic cable is wrapped around the boom arm. This helps guard against the mic falling to the ground if, for some reason, it comes detached from the shock mount. This is a really cool safety feature.

GOBOS AND ROOM ACOUSTICS

Sometimes we forget how important the sound of the room we place the microphone in truly is—it's everything. The best microphone won't give you good results if it's placed in a bad-sounding room.

Even when the room sounds great, we still need to shape the sound at the microphone by controlling how much of that room is heard in the recording. The most commonly used tool for this purpose is called a "gobo," which is short for "go-between." Gobos can actually create a small room within a larger room. A typical gobo consists of a wooden wall—often cedar or some other soft wood—covered on one side with an absorptive material such as Owens Corning 702 or 703 fiberglass insulation. Gobos don't do a very good job controlling low frequencies below about 200–400 Hz (depending on the physical size of the gobo). But they do a good job controlling higher-frequency acoustic reflections.

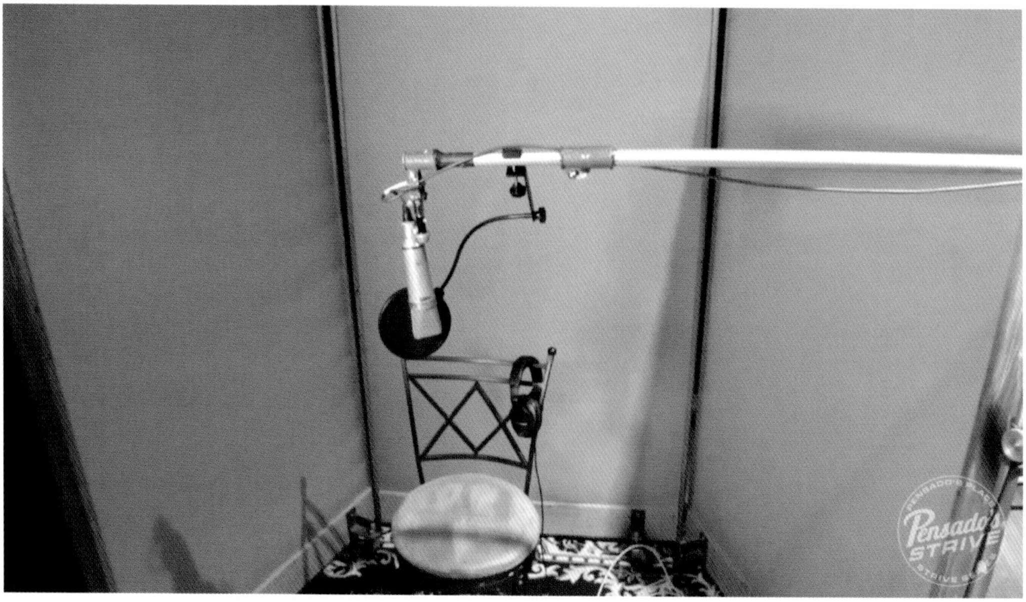

This room at the Record Plant in Los Angeles has a large live feel to it. Notice that the microphone is surrounded by gobos. This is done to control the amount of room ambience that's picked up by the mic.

If you don't have gobos and don't have the material, ability, or funding to make them, try experimenting with materials that you have on hand, like duvet covers, blankets, sofa cushions, and so on. Use anything you can to shrink the space around the mic. It's all about minimizing the influence of reflections from around the room.

Low-frequency information is really difficult to control. If you're not getting the sound on the vocal you want and you've tried using various types of materials around the mic to shape the sound, you probably have a low-frequency issue in the room. Now, don't go buy (unless you have a little extra cash) some of the foam acoustical panels you see advertised and expect them to solve your problem. They do a great job controlling high-end reflections but they don't control the low end—they're not going to make your room sound like the Record Plant.

POSITIONING MONITORS

Sometimes it's not the studio design that's causing the problems you hear through your monitors. It may simply be the location of your monitors in the control room. Have two friends move the speakers for you while you're monitoring. If your control room is not specifically designed for a balanced frequency response, it makes a big difference how close your monitors are to the back wall behind the console, the side walls, and how far they are from your prime listening position. In the same way that a microphone is only as good as the room that it's in, you are only as good as your mixing environment. You must be able to trust the sound of the studio, the mic, and the monitors in your control room.

3

Mic Selection

Mic selection is extremely important. Back in the old days, when equalizers weren't as sophisticated as they are now and we didn't have the tools we have now, mic selection was the main way to affect the recorded sound. Mic selection and technique are no less important today than they were back then. The important thing to understand about mic selection is that you can read about it and you can listen to my tutorials, but to really master it, you just have to check out as many microphones as you can in as many circumstances as you can and you need to log the results of those combinations in your memory. Through that continual process, you'll establish a vocabulary of microphones you can choose from when you're looking for a certain sound.

I'm giving you guidelines about specific microphones so you'll get a feel for the thought process that's involved in selecting them. I'm not suggesting that you go buy these microphones or that you only use them in the ways I'm describing. Consider what we've discussed so far. Use what you know about the different mics to guide your choices but don't be afraid to mix it up. There's no harm miking a male rapper using a pristine signal path you might normally use for a female singer—there's nothing that says that won't work. And always be on the lookout for happy accidents. They're more prevalent than you might think.

MIKING LEAD VOCALS

Working with a female lead singer, I'd typically go with a mic that has a larger diaphragm, like the Telefunken 251. If I'm working with a male lead vocalist, often I'll use the Manley Labs Reference Cardioid Microphone. It's an amazing mic and it's used on a lot of big records.

When I'm recording a hip-hop artist, I'll often use a combination of a Shure SM7B and a good large-diaphragm condenser mic. I set them up so there are no phase issues—so the mic capsules are lined up perfectly with each other—and I'll usually record them to separate tracks. I like this approach because I like the proximity effect on the SM7B. It gives a rapper just a great aggressive tone.

To avoid phase problems when recording a singer with two mics at the same time, always make sure the capsules line up perfectly on the same plane in front of the singer.

Some singers sound great on a Sony C800, which is a very expensive microphone. There's another microphone by David Pearlman (Pearlman Microphones TM-47) that emulates a Neumann U 47. It's very affordable (under $2000) and I own one. I love that microphone.

For metal and rock singers, most of the time I'll use an SM7B because it can handle a lot of level; however, I'd record them with a condenser at the same time to get as much high end as I want during mixdown. You can actually get a lot of high end out of an SM7B but you have to be careful that you're at the spot in the room where the high frequencies aren't cancelling out. If the microphone is in the wrong spot in the room, the highs can cancel out quite easily.

I've recorded rap vocalists with so many microphones. I like large-diaphragm condensers more than small-diaphragm condensers. Another mic that comes to mind for recording rap vocals is the Neumann U 87, especially if you can get one that's been modified by Klaus Heine or Stephen Paul (1951–2003). They're very, very good. And again, don't be afraid to use your old buddy the SM7B, which—as you can see throughout this book—is like the "island microphone." You know, if you could take one microphone to a desert island…

BACKGROUND VOCALS

Background vocals are a little bit different because of the way we record them. Sometimes the same singer will record twenty or more background vocal tracks. I don't like to just set up one microphone and record all twenty vocals. That approach can homogenize the sound and pasteurize it so it sounds a little too smooth. I like to change microphones occasionally. I might do the low notes with the SM7, and as we stack up more of the higher notes, I might move to condenser microphones.

When I'm recording a group of people singing backgrounds, which often happens, I've got to make a choice, usually between a stereo technique like an MS or Blumlein technique. With either of those configurations on a group of singers, I'd use condenser mics.

Choirs are a unique situation. I tend to mic them as I would a string section. When you've got one singer, you've got the sound in one little spot, but when you're miking a choir, you've got a very expansive sound source that might be twenty feet wide.

If I only had one microphone to record a choir, I would use an omnidirectional large-diaphragm condenser mic. But if I had two microphones that were the same, I would think about an X-Y—or an MS pair if I had microphones with different patterns—or I might consider using a Blumlein configuration.

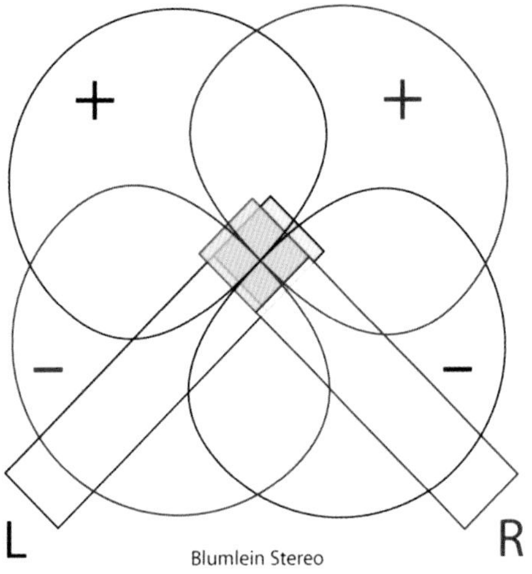

Blumlein stereo mic configuration

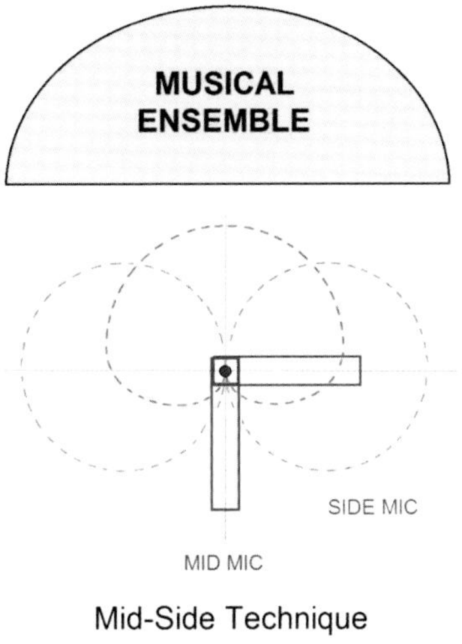

Mid-Side (MS) stereo mic configuration

As another option, I might place one on the right side, one on the left side, and then go back in the control room and listen. To find the best positions for the mics, try walking around the room while listening to the mics through headphones. You'll find the best sound pretty quickly this way. You might need to move some of the louder people back and some of the softer people forward. Recording choirs is always a science project, plus you've got to keep them excited while you find the right sound—that's really important, too!

4

Getting Ready to Record

The process of recording vocals starts the minute the client walks into the studio. In this chapter, I'm going to show you some techniques that will help make recording vocals a pleasant experience. These techniques will help you project the kind of credibility and confidence that will make the vocalist feel comfortable and secure enough to give their very best performance.

MAKING A VOCALIST FEEL COMFORTABLE

Probably the best way to make a vocalist feel comfortable is to simply follow the golden rule. Think about how you would like to be treated if you were walking into a strange room with a bunch of people you don't know staring at you and expecting you to suddenly sing a perfect take. What would you like to have happen if you were the singer? For me, I'd like the experience to start way before I even enter the studio, with an extremely nice receptionist who greets me at the door. And I'd like to feel like people are expecting me. I'm not a singer, but if I were a singer that's what I'd like to have happen. When I'm working in a studio, that's what I try to provide for vocalists that I record. I'll buy the receptionist lunch and dinner just to get her on my side so that when my clients show up he or she will be pleasant and nice. Actually, you can probably save your money because professional studios are that way all the time but that's just what I like to do.

I do everything I can to make sure the vocalist has a very positive experience in the studio. I'll research her favorite mics and have them set up along with a few others to try out. I make sure the receptionist is expecting her and that she receives the royal treatment. Hopefully, that helps the singer have confidence in me but it's really all about building her confidence in herself and her surroundings so she's free to sing her very best.

All singers are insecure when they hear their voice soloed—they don't like having strangers listen to their voice. I can name you some great singers I've worked with and you'd think they wouldn't be this way but they're just as insecure as the rest of us. I don't know why. I guess it's because when you hear your voice played back it always sounds different to you than when you're listening to it inside your head. So try and get everything possible in place to make the vocalist comfortable during the recording process.

When the singer comes into the control room, remember you have the power of the chair. Just the fact that you're an engineer sitting in that chair gives the singer the feeling you must know what you're doing. Use that. Be confident. Talk in concrete terms.

I would never ask a singer what their favorite mic is. I would look at some records to see the names of the studios they've worked at. Then I'd call those engineers and politely ask them what the singer's favorite mic was. Sometimes they'll tell me, sometimes they won't. In any case, do your research and try to find out what mics the singer likes, then have a selection to choose from that includes those mics. Have everything set up in advance. This is all about doing what it takes to give them confidence in you, the studio, and ultimately in themselves.

I've worked with a producer named Rhett Lawrence. Rhett has done more hits with more female singers than anyone. He had this technique where he'd hide magazines with another singer's face on the cover. He'd make sure the singer walked in and didn't see any other singers, because even that slight feeling of competition might create an insecurity, which could get in the way of a truly great performance. Rhett has his singers just come into the studio and immediately start recording. A recording engineer needs to have a good bedside manner, just like a doctor, or a hairstylist, or like anybody in any other service industry. And be assured, we are a service industry.

Rhett Lawrence knows the importance of providing a stress-free environment for the singers he produces. He pays attention to the smallest of details that might emotionally impact a singer, from setting the right mood with lighting to making sure there aren't magazines or photos around the studio that highlight other singers.

Make a good first impression. It's incredibly important and it starts the pattern of building the singer's confidence in you. And use your imagination in how you build a relationship with the vocalists you record. Create some techniques that suit your personality. But don't talk too much. The more you talk, the more you give away that you're not the best engineer in the world. It's the same for me. I don't talk much when I'm working with a singer, initially. It's enough to be cordial, but they're there to work and so are you.

5

Planning for the Session

You can't just walk in cold to a vocal session and expect to get the best results. You need to plan ahead and create an environment that helps the singer feel relaxed. He or she needs to be confident that you know what you're doing and that you care about the project.

THE LYRIC SHEET

It might seem kind of mundane and obvious but if you're not given a lyric sheet, create your own from the demo. Create the lyric sheet in such a way that you can easily navigate to different points in the song. I mark the measure and beat number at the beginning of every phrase. If the singer says, "Can I do the second line of the third verse?" Blam-O! You're there! Or, "Can you do that third ad-lib in the vamp?" Bam! You're there. I use the margin on the left side of the lyric sheet to mark the bar numbers for the start of each phrase. The lyric sheet is such an important tool!

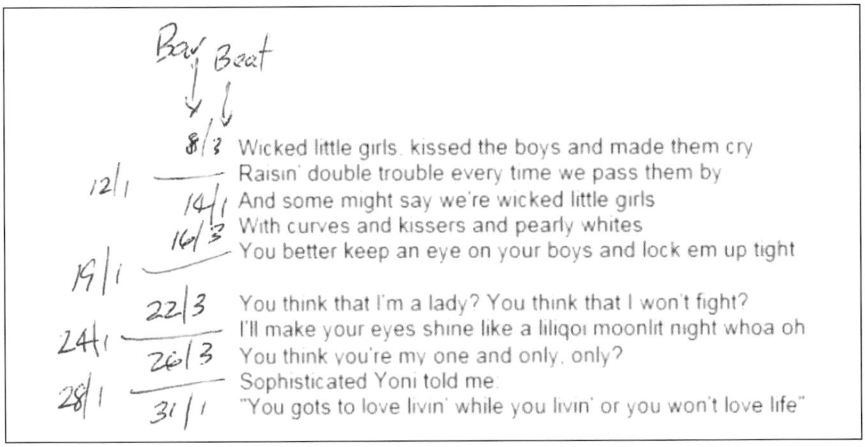

Bar Beat

8/3 Wicked little girls, kissed the boys and made them cry
12/1 Raisin' double trouble every time we pass them by
14/1 And some might say we're wicked little girls
16/3 With curves and kissers and pearly whites
19/1 You better keep an eye on your boys and lock em up tight

22/3 You think that I'm a lady? You think that I won't fight?
24/1 I'll make your eyes shine like a liliqoi moonlit night whoa oh
26/3 You think you're my one and only, only?
28/1 Sophisticated Yoni told me:
31/1 "You gots to love livin' while you livin' or you won't love life"

Always use a lyric sheet. Mark the start point of each phrase in the left hand margin so you're always ready to go right to any spot in the song.

Look for a line in the lyrics that you really like. When the singer walks in, say something like, "Man, the first line of the second verse just grabs me," and then repeat the line from memory. It gives them confidence that you've done your homework and that you're into the project.

THE DEMO

The demo is the greatest source of information you're going to ever have. Study it like crazy. You can learn a lot from the demo. You're going to learn which microphones you would expect to sound good based on your previous experience selecting microphones for other similar-sounding artists. If there's a lot of loud parts and a lot of dynamics, you might select an SM7B. Or, depending on the song, you might select a condenser. The demo is going to provide insight into how to select the microphones. If you're hearing a lot of background vocals, you'll need to have your plan for recording background vocals ready to go. Figure out how many headphones and headphone mixes you'll need. A lot of times I'll listen to the rough mix through the headphones, and then I'll go out into the room where we're going to record and set up the singer's mix so that it sounds like the rough mix through the headphones that he or she will be using.

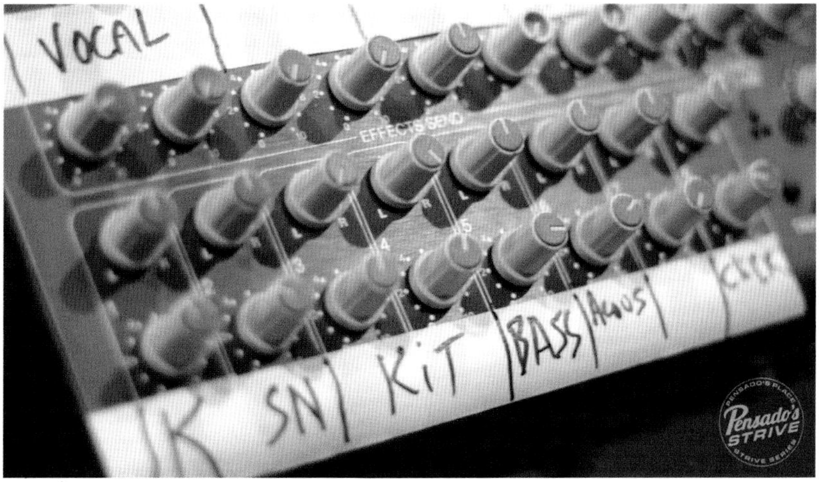

I make it a point to set up the singer's headphone mix so it sounds like the rough mix she's been listening to in preparation for the session.

When the session starts, I've already taken notes on that specific singer, I have all my levels approximated, and the effects are set up. If the singer has been listening to the rough mix with reverb on the vocals for six weeks, I'll definitely have a similar reverb ready for her headphones. Now she can just walk in and sing.

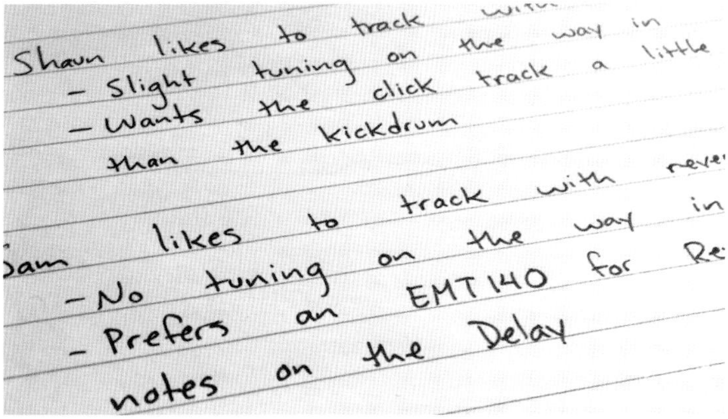

Before the session starts, I already have notes on what the singer likes, maybe from the rough mix or talking to her, or if I've worked with her before, from previous sessions.

Have everything you possibly can ready to go. I can't over-emphasize it. The demo can give you what you need to know about how to proceed and how to have the session ready. I promise you, when you do the things in this category, it gives the singer a great feeling of self-confidence. They feel like they can sing whatever they want and you're going to be that safety net that catches them. They trust that you'll never let anything leave the room that might embarrass them. And because of all that confidence, you get a better performance!

HEADPHONES

Headphones are probably the most underutilized tool in the recording engineer's arsenal. If you use the headphones properly, you can be very helpful during the recording process. First have all of your effects set and ready to go. I like to make sure I listen to early takes of the singer when they're available. I listen to their timing. If the timing is a bit erratic, I'm going to kick the drums up in their headphone mix. If they're struggling with pitch, I might pull the drums back a little bit and turn some of the harmonic elements up. For example, if there's a big piano part, I might take everything down but that piano and the drums. I'll emphasize parts of the music in the singer's headphones that I expect will help him or her deliver a better performance.

I've had a lot of practice trying to help singers deliver their best performances. Here are a few things I've discovered:

- Sometimes a little reverb will make a singer sing sharp or flat, so if you're having a pitch problem, increase or decrease the reverb.
- Singers tend to sing a little sharp as they get older. Younger singers tend to sing flat. Sometimes you can counteract these tendencies by adjusting the amount of reverb in the phones.
- Make sure the headphones are perfect when the singer walks into the studio. He or she will subconsciously think you're a great engineer when they hear a great mix in the headphones from the start. They're just perfect. I had a number one record with Brian McKnight and he didn't warm up. He walked in, sang the song, it went to tape, out the door and number one in a month. That's what you want to be able to do.

- Always take notes about where you place the mic, what mic you used, and the exact levels for all parameters on any outboard hardware that you've used. That way the next time that singer comes in, you're ready to go with the precise sound you previously constructed.
- This is a technique that I'm pretty sure other people do—I like using this and I use it a lot. I'm actually kind of scared to tell you guys, so if you know any singers that know me, don't tell them this. I set the level of the headphone mix a little lower than it should be while the singer is warming up and even when we're recording the initial takes. But when I think we're getting close to a good take, I'll kick the headphone level up three decibels. It juices their headphones! They're more comfortable, they love me, the headphones are hot, the lights are right, the tea is perfect, and man, I've just captured the greatest performance in the world.
- Train yourself to look for characteristics that are unique to each singer. Look for ways to capitalize on those characteristics in a way that enhances the recording experience and helps them sing better. That's why you're sitting in the engineer's chair! You're not there just to make sure the levels are correct. You're there to do everything you can capture the best possible performances.

I see a lot of engineers who wear a singer out just testing a microphone setup. That's very destructive. By the time the engineer is through testing the gear, the singer has lost the excitement and energy that comes with just showing up at the studio. If you're working with an excellent female vocalist, for example, find an up-and-coming singer who has a similar style and offer to record some of her vocals for free if she'll come sing for you while you dial in the sounds. Now you've got a free guinea pig to help out while you set microphones, levels, EQ, and so on, and she walks home with a free performance. Now you're ready to go when your big star singer comes in. She'll think you're the best engineer and everybody benefits because you're ready to capture her most excited, enthusiastic, and fresh performances.

Think about these things that I'm recommending, but most of all, use this kind of mindset to create your own techniques.

KNOWING HOW TO GET A GREAT VOCAL

Study the singers you work with. It's important that you get a feel for certain tendencies they have. You might notice things they could do better. Analyze those things. You might be able to help enhance their performance in some way. Here are a few techniques I've discovered to help get a better performance from a singer:

- For example, a lot of singers slouch over when they sing, which restricts their air pipe. Singing is just moving air through your vocal cords, so if the singer has a restricted air pipe, he or she won't be able to get to the right notes. The singer might also tend to go flat at the end of a long word or phrase because they just run out of air. Encourage the singer to use better posture. Always think Lemmy Kilmister from Motorhead. He's got the mic way up in the air so he has to aim upward to sing into it! From his mouth, down his throat, to his lungs it's almost straight down. If he were crouched over, there'd be a restriction in his airflow. Posture is important. Find techniques that you're comfortable with suggesting to the singer, especially if they're running out of air.
- Sometimes I can get a good performance out of a singer if I make them smile. I ask them to smile or I might tell a joke and say, "Oh man, let's cut it with that smile. That's going to be the take." I don't know why that works—it doesn't work with everyone—but here again, you want to find techniques that you can suggest to help improve the singer's performance. If a singer is having some problems I might suggest, "Sing from your diaphragm." Even though I'm not a singer, I know that singing from the diaphragm is important and when I remind a singer about it, it sometimes helps. Try it.
- I like to tell singers to relax their throat. It's simple. When you get in front of a crowd and you're a little nervous, your voice sounds different. Can you imagine being a singer and you're out there all by yourself? You don't have a guitar to hide behind. You don't have a drum kit to hide behind. If you make a bad sound, it's you. I can look down at my guitar and blame it on the guitar, but for singers, it's all them. So find ways to get them to relax their throat and suggest they try moving more air when they sing.

- Singers such as Mariah Carey and Christina Aguilera move so much air when they sing that you can hear it when you mix their stuff. Because they're great, and they move a lot of air when they sing, I figure that suggesting the singers move a lot of air might just help them get a little more out of what they're doing.
- I was working with a singer one time and I said, "Man, you didn't quite hit the note." He stayed silent forever and I thought: Wow, I made a mistake. Then he said, "Dave, I don't hit notes. I just sing." Sometimes, it's best to just encourage the singer to just sing. I mean, that's what they do. Great singers are singing all the time, so just tell them to sing. Say, "Don't sing the words. Sing the song. You know, sell me on the song. Convince me." Then dim the lights and make sure everyone in the control room is paying attention. If there's anybody in the control room laughing and not looking at the singer, then the singer is going to automatically think they're being laughed at or that they're not doing a good job. Make sure you control all the people in the room. When the singer comes back into the control room, get everyone to cheer. You want to prop that singer up. You can't just say, "Do what I tell you." You've got to be extremely subtle.
- Try to get the singer to memorize the lyrics. If they memorize the lyrics, it's always going to be a better performance. The more the singers have the lyrics committed to memory, the more they can put their personality into the performance. There are some exceptions to that rule. I worked on a song with Christina, and the first time she sang it, she nailed it. That's the take that ended up on the record. I mean that woman's amazing! The song's called "Beautiful."
- You can't do this with all singers, but if you've got a good relationship and you're close to the singer, suggest they perform—that they put themselves on stage. Rent some lights and get a vibe in the room they're accustomed to. Try to minimize the sterile and foreign environment that the studio can often represent. It can make a big difference with some singers!

I'm sure you guys are going to come up with all sorts of techniques that work well. And by the way, if you're recording yourself, this stuff works on you too!

6

Vocal Recording Chain

When I first started recording vocals, I made a lot of mistakes. One of the less obvious things that stood between me and perfect vocal recordings was the gain structure for everything along the signal path. The microphone, the output of the microphone, the mic pre, the line amps, the impedance, and all that kind of stuff is extremely important. These are all factors that are very subtle, and a little nebulous, but they are so, so, so important.

MIC PRE

One of the things, among many, that took me a while to understand is that the microphone puts out a very small signal—a very low amperage—and you must amplify that signal before it gets to the console. And there other places along the signal path where the signal gets amplified or padded down. We call that pathway the "signal chain." It starts with the microphone and it ends with whatever the recording medium you're using. A lot of people think that if you're using a tube mic, you shouldn't use a tube-based mic preamplifier. Or, to put it differently, if you've got a tube mic preamplifier, you shouldn't use a tube mic. I'm a big believer in just experimenting. There are some combinations that just seem to work. The combination that's most classic is a Neumann U 47 or a Telefunken 251 microphone through a Neve 1073 preamp—now that's an amazing sound! But what if you want to be unique? Don't hesitate to try different combinations. Even a very inexpensive mic through a really expensive mic preamp can give you a cool sound, or vice versa. The main thing that you need to listen for is the microphone—the capsule itself. When it's responding to pressure, it can wrinkle and cause distortion. If you've got a microphone with a separate power supply that controls the output level, it's possible you're sending too much level from the mic to the preamp.

Impedance is an important consideration but you don't necessarily need to know all about electrical theory. However, you do need to trust your ears to recognize when there's a problem. Then you need to find a way to fix it. If you're hearing certain irregularities in the vocal—the catch all phrase is "distortion"—first experiment with the singer. Maybe the singer is singing too close to the mic, in which case you might have to use a pop filter or you might need to ask the singer to move back from the mic a little bit. And if that doesn't solve the problem, check the input to the mic preamplifier. On most mic preamps you can adjust the amplification for the microphone signal into the preamp and you can also adjust the preamp output level to the recorder. There are several places in the signal chain that can make or break the sound you want to record. I've been doing this a long time and I can't always predict when there's going to be a problem. This is one area where you have to try a few things and memorize the solutions you uncover in your particular environment.

COMPRESSORS

The conundrum: should I record compressors and equalizers to the DAW or should I record flat and add compression and EQ later. I'm a firm believer in commitment. I really believe that if you're not ready to commit, you're not ready to record. So, if I decide to record compression to the DAW track, I might use a gentle compression. Back in the day, we had to use compression going to reel-to-reel tape because if we didn't get the signal printed strong enough to tape and then we turned that signal up in the mix, we're not only turning the signal we recorded, we were also turning up all the background noise (hiss) the tape itself generated. It was very important to record everything as loud as possible to tape just to stay as far as possible away from the noise floor. Now in the world of the DAW, we originally thought that if you didn't record hot enough, you wouldn't get efficient use of all the bits. For example, if you recorded kind of low in a 24-bit world, you might only get the recording quality of 16 bits. Don't worry about that, just don't worry about it.

Having said all that, I like to use a very low ratio—2:1 or 3:1 at the most—and a slow attack time. Then I set the release time based on the tempo. I'm very careful to make sure that I can't hear the compressor working. In the digital world, it's easy to record both. You can record one track through the compressor, and at the same time, record a track without the compressor.

There are several incredible hardware compressors. The UREI 1176LN Limiting Amplifier is the granddaddy of them all. But there are several excellent newer compressors, like the Tube-Tech CL 1B, the Avalon Design AD2044, Shadow Hills makes some great compressors, and I'm using one called the Locomotive Audio 14B that I like a lot right now—it's just a great sounding vocal compressor. I tend to use more compression in the mixing part of the process than the recording part, but sometimes you want to hear how the track is going to sit in the mix, so I like to commit to a little bit of gentle compression. Also, I like to hear the coloration I get with different types of compressors.

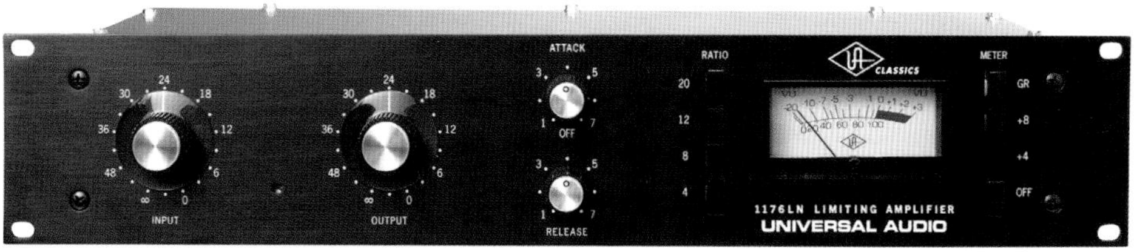

The UREI 1176LN Limiting Amplifier

The Tube-Tech Compressor CL 1B

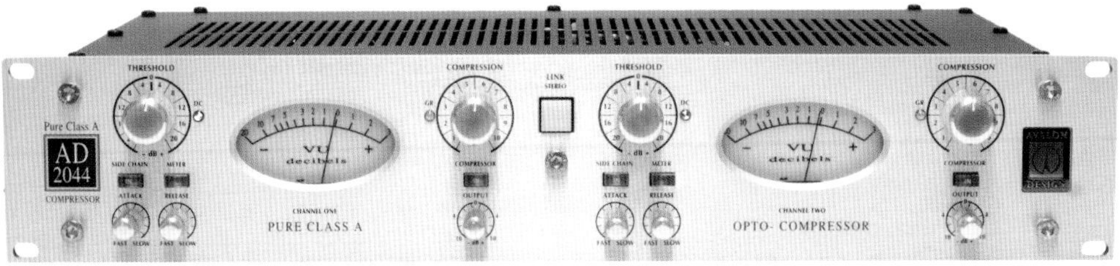

The Avalon Design AD2044 Pure Class A/Opto Compressor

The Shadow Hills Industries Mastering Compressor

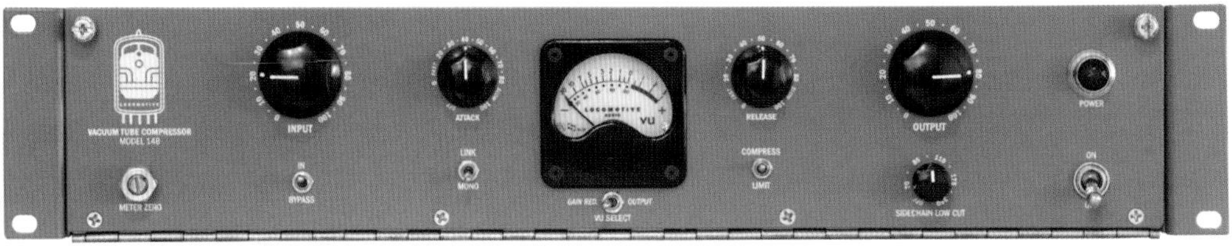

The Locomotive Vacuum Tube Compressor, Model 14B

Don't be afraid to use plug-ins as you record. You'll need to be careful about latency issues but with newer computers and interfaces, that's not too much of a problem. In the plug-in world, there are so many great options. I love the Klanghelm MJUC. And, I love the Audified U73b compressor. The UAD compressors are really great, in particular the 1176. Waves makes some great compressor plug-ins, too. It's just hard to find a bad plug-in compressor. Compression is your friend and it definitely has a use. It's hard to anticipate what style of compression you'll need and want until you put the track in the mix.

The Klanghelm MJUC variable-tube compressor

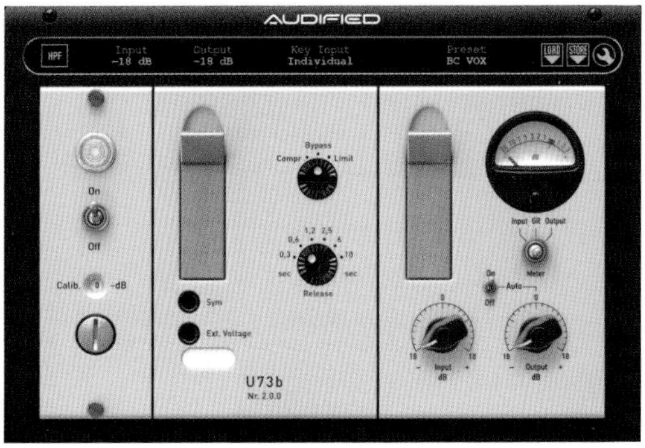

The Audified U73b compressor

Three vintages of the UAD 1176 compressor plug-in:
Rev A, Rev e, and AE

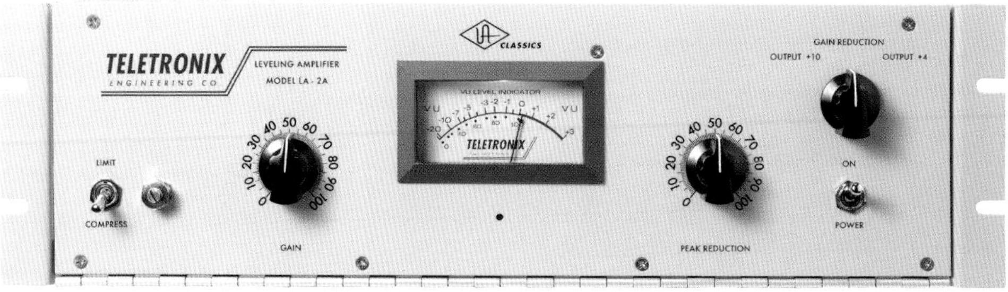

The Teletronix Leveling Amplifier Model LA 2A from Universal Audio

EQ

Applying equalization is one of my favorite things to do. I like equalizing. A lot of times I have to take the EQ off but sometimes I find some cool things by experimenting. When recording vocals and printing the EQ to the track, be careful—and it's hard for me to say "be careful." It's okay to take out some of the mud from the bottom and it's okay to tame a little bit of the high end but just make sure you're not creating a problem that you'll need to struggle to repair in the mix.

In the hardware world, the GML 8200 5-band stereo parametric EQ is just wonderful. The Avalon Design AD2055 is just amazing! But, you're saying to yourself, "Dave! What about a 1073." I don't use 1073s too much because everybody uses them. It's hard to separate yourself from the pack when you use what everybody is using. Also, the Neve 1073 is great but it's older technology so you don't get access to all the EQ points you want. Back when the 1073 was new, if you had access to 3, 4, 5, 8, 10, and 16 kHz you were happy. But nowadays we work in smaller increments. But if that's your thing and you've got one, please use it. It's an amazing piece of gear. I tend to like parametric equalizers. The Millennia NSEQ-2 is a good equalizer for tracking.

The George Massenburg Labs GML 8200 Parametric Equalizer

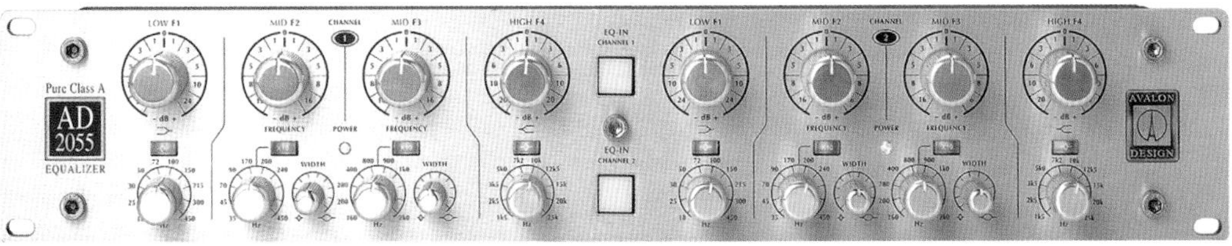

The Avalon Design AD2055 Pure Class A Equalizer

The Classic Neve 1073 Mic Preamp and Equalizer

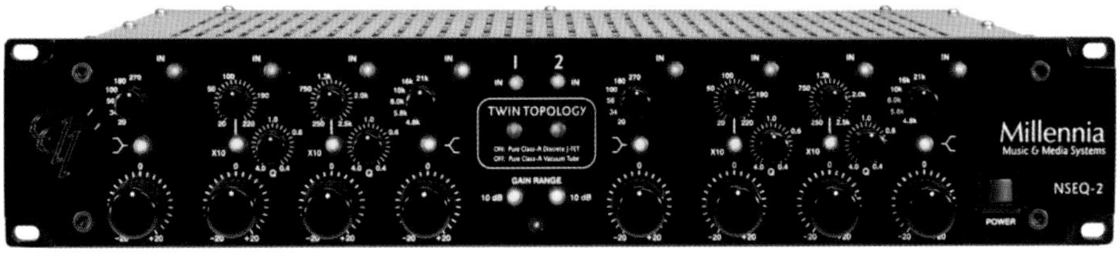

The Millennia Media NSEQ-2 Twin Topology Two Channel Parametric EQ

During tracking I will commit to a sound or coloration I like, so the Neve 1073 would qualify for that, as would some of the API preamp/EQs. In the mix, coming off the recorder, I would do something different. For tracking through plug-ins, there are several that I like a lot. I like the Massenburg Design Works 5 from UAD. I love the new IK Multimedia T-RackS Master EQ 432—it's a great copy of the PrismSound Masalec MEA-2 Mastering Equalizer, which is a great, great EQ with a super top-end on it. I also love the top-end on the Fabrice Gabriel's Eiosis Air EQ. I love Cliff Maag's EQ4—I use it on everything.

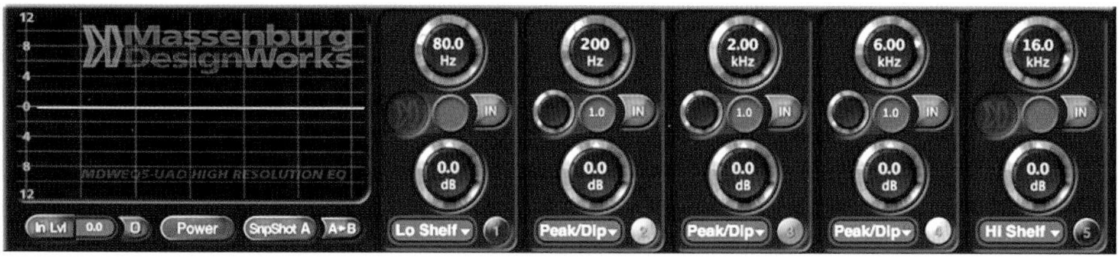

The Massenburg Design Works MDWEQ5 Parametric Equalizer

The IK Multimedia T-RackS Master EQ 432

The PrismSound Masalec Master Series MEA-2 precision stereo equalizer

The Fabrice Gabriel Eiosis AirEQ

The Mäag Audio EQ4M

Use EQ judiciously. Maybe clear out some of the mud and when you're equalizing during tracking, make sure you've got a fairly accurate representation of the mix that the vocal is going to sit in. And be patient and smart. Try to wait until the mix process to make your final choices. I don't always have that kind of self-control but I can bail myself out pretty easily most of the time. Knowing how to use EQ is a necessary thing.

7

Recording a Vocal

Watch the video segment that follows. You'll see a vocal tracking session in Los Angeles at the Record Plant—a studio I love. The session takes place in a room where Ron Fair and I worked a lot. Ron practically lived in this room. You're going to see some cool things in this video segment and I really want to give a shout out to Jeff Barnes for letting us shoot this session at the world-famous Record Plant.

THE VOCAL SESSION

Watch Leandro Hidalgo, my assistant, recording Esthero, one of my favorite artists ever: http://content.groove3.com/videos/VocalSessionAtTheRecordPlantWithLeandroHidalgo.mp4. She's an amazing singer. I want you to pay close attention to the interaction between Esthero and Leandro. A lot of the things that I've described, so far, are displayed here. These interactions are subtle so you might need to run this several times to catch everything.

Esthero loves the Neumann U 87. Notice how she responds and sings through that microphone. She's not so fond of the Shure SM7, but I wanted to put a couple mics up so you could see how a great singer responds to each one. In a perfect world, I might use a little bit of both.

INTERVIEW: DAVE PENSADO WITH ESTHERO

Dave Pensado: ***Esthero, thanks for helping out with this book! For those of you who aren't familiar with Esthero, you should look her up. You wrote three songs on Kanye's*** **808s & Heartbreak*****, right?***

Esthero: Yeah, co-wrote.

And sang on a lot of other stuff. She's sung with Dre and she's been on **Grey's Anatomy.**

Got a lot of film and TV placements and stuff like that.

You're amazing. I've known you since you were 18. We did a record together and it's still one of my favorite albums I've ever done. If you know anybody from Toronto, tell them you're watching Esthero and they'll be like, "Oh, my god! I love Esthero." I do that all the time. When I need credibility with somebody from Toronto, I tell them I know you [**laughing*****]. She's not going to say this but Esthero has got, I don't know if you'd describe it as perfect pitch, but her pitch and timing are immaculate. She can sing something, leave town, come back, and sing it again without hearing it and make it flange. It's like nothing you've ever seen. So, tell the Dre story.***

I was in the studio with Dre. I was just hanging out and he was working on something. I think it was for a game or maybe it was for him. It eventually ended up being like something that the game released but I was just hanging out and I heard this part that he was doing. It was called "Makeup Sex." I remember because it was like, "No apologies necessary; Let's get that missionary; It's time wind down and get ready for some oooo." I remember I had an idea and I just looked at Dre and I was like, "Would it be okay if I sang on this?" And he was like, "Go ahead." He was really lovely about it. He was like, "Yeah, go ahead. Go try something." In my mind before

I go in and do a vocal, I can kind of calculate how many stacks I'm going to do of a lead, how many harmonies I'm going to do, how many moving harmonies I'm going to do, and I like to give an engineer a break. I'm a little bit Rain Man about it. Before I walk into a booth, I go like, "Open up 16 tracks," so that they're ready to go and the engineer doesn't have to scramble to keep up. So, I walked in and when I double, I do this thing called, "doubling blind." A lot of people double their vocals and have the previous vocal playing at the same time in their headphones. I actually find that extremely distracting. I'll sing a vocal and then I'm like, "Okay, two." And then, "Okay, three."

***So you weren't even hearing the previous takes*?**

No, and I'm just like next, next, next.

You have perfect time and perfect pitch.

So basically, after I've layered four or five tracks, I see Dre walk over to the engineer who, even though the talkback is off, I can tell motions to Dre to hold on for just a second. I knew what he was doing because most people aren't used to singers doubling blind. They're always listening back to the one they did and he wanted the engineer to play it back to check it. And before he leaned over I just—you know my ego—I said, "If you're checking to see if it's going to be okay, like I have to do more than four because it's going to be so perfect it will phase."

I know that for a fact.

And he got this kind of look on his face like, "Whatever." And he's like [*motions okay*] and I saw him press play and I saw his face go [*silently*], "What the fuck?" And it was like, "Continue" [*laughing*]. And then later on, Xzibit came in the studio and it made me so happy because Dre was kind of like bragging about it. Man, you know like you do your X's and she was like they're perfect. She's not even listening to the one she did before. But it's really just a party trick I think. Ultimately, people grow up getting used to the idea that they're supposed to have one ear on or both ears in the headphones. But for me, it's not like a superpower so much. The part of it where my pitch memory and my muscle memory of what my voice is doing in each vocal—maybe that's a skill—but as far as not hearing it, it's actually easier. It's too hard for the brain to listen to what you did before and listen to what you're doing now.

A normal person would want some advice about how to double vocals and how to stack 16 tracks of backgrounds. I mean, have you always done it that way?

Yeah, I think it's different for each person. From the moment I was in a studio starting to double things, which I'm not generally a fan of, I didn't like to double lead vocals. That's just my particular production style. I find that lead vocals sound bigger on their own, anyway. I like to just throw a bunch of reverb on everything and then for me the stacks I like to do are on background vocals or like a couple words on things. But I know that from the beginning, being very young and in my very early experiences in studios, people were always wanting to play the first track back and I'd be like, "Can you turn it off because when it's on, I go pitchy." Some people need it there as a guide and I would just suggest keeping it extremely low. But a lot of the time, doubling on lead vocals sucks all the character out of it. I really keep doubling for big stacked background vocals and stuff like that.

So, in general when you're stacking background vocals, do you like to do root, third fifth—or something in that—and then do four notes of each? Two left and two right?

It just depends what the section is. Usually it's like the third of whatever the lead vocal was but I'll do the main note that I want everyone to hear. Sometimes I'll stack four and sometimes I'll stack six. If I'm doing four, I'm generally splitting them apart, and if I'm doing six, it's so that I can have two on each side and two up the middle. That's just how I like to do things. And then I'll keep that main note with everything in the middle and then when I do the third above that—like the next high harmony—I usually do the same thing, recording four to six doubles, depending on what the situation calls for. I like to split the vocal tracks about like a 45-degree angle apart. So, if I do two tracks on one side and two on the other, I very rarely do hard pans. I do like a kinda to the right, kinda to the right and then…

Kinda to the right, right [**laughing*****]?***

Yeah [*laughing*]. Then I usually set the highest harmony at the quietest volume and I usually do four to six of those, depending on how smooth I need it to be and how high the note is for me. More tracks will obviously hide any mistakes. If you can double it perfectly and everything is in your range, you can get that sort of perfection. Then it's okay to split them up but for me when things are slightly different and they're noticeably off, the more you separate them, the more you're going to hear the differences, so it's better for me to just keep them in the middle. Whenever I'm doing a low harmony underneath anything low, I usually only do two of those.

I've mixed stuff for you in every genre. Do you do backgrounds a little differently depending on the genre? In some R&B songs, the background vocals become the lead and the lead ad libs around that. But in a rock song the lead stays the lead but the background vocals are just a couple small notes underneath.

Exactly. If I'm doing something that's got an R&B, or kind of a sexy time feel or whatever, I try to make that as tight as possible. It's super stacked, it's super sheeny, and then if I'm doing something that's little more punk rock, or full of character, it'll just be one harmony and I might intentionally not do them perfect. I feel like, especially rock and roll, is about the imperfection. And punk rock is more about the tone that you're getting, you know?

When you're recording, I watch your face and you just go to another place. Not all engineers can handle something like that without destroying the moment trying to get the technical stuff right. What are the qualities you look for in an engineer that can enhance your performance?

Number one is presence, staying with me and being as invested as I am. It's a lot to ask of somebody who didn't write the music, but whatever engineer I'm working with is an extension of me. When I'm doing vocals, especially really emotional stuff, I need you to stay with me because I'm often doing things that are extremely emotional—things that I'm really attached to and invested in emotionally. There's nothing worse than being with an engineer and trying to get it out—especially if things are going really well—and I'm like, back it up to the second line and they're sitting there going, "Which one was that?" I need you to be with me.

It destroys everything!

Yeah, and I'm like, "Why are you not here with me, listening to me. This is going to take so much longer than it should." For me, there's nothing worse than an engineer that's only there to push buttons and space out. I want you to be a member of my band, temporarily. I want you to participate with me. So that's my favorite thing, when I get engineers that are on it. They're ready to go. They're invested with you. Even in their feedback they're like, "Wow, that line was really cool," or like, "You might have been slightly pitchy." That's the number one quality I look for in an engineer: somebody who's just present with me the whole time. That's a lot to ask of somebody but it's the nature of the game, right?

Anyone reading this who wants to earn a living doing this, please reread what Esthero just said and feel the passion with which she said it. There are different types of people who come into the recording studio to do vocals. Some like to be led and some like to do the leading. It's a juggling act. You've always got six little balls in the air juggling, juggling, juggling. When things stop, they all just hit the ground and you've gotta start all over again. So, sit down with a singer before he or she even starts singing or rapping and get a feel for how they work. And just be candid. If you're a new engineer starting out, don't try to fake it—it won't work. I tried, it didn't work for me when I first started. Just say, "Look, I haven't done that many sessions. I need your help."

I usually walk into the room and I'm like, here's my shorthand. If I start doing a stack, I want to do them quickly. If I say, "okay" or "next," that means, move on to the next one. If I say "again" that means erase what I just did and I want to do it again. If I say "one more time," it means I hate what I just did. I also really appreciate an engineer who will listen to me—this is a big thing for me. I am a Capricorn and I'm also from a side where I'm generally producing. I'm not just singing, I'm also producing the track. A big thing for me is that I hate clutter. I hate it when there's too much to choose from. Also, I'm confident enough in my ability that if I didn't get it on one take, I know that I will get it right at some point. I know that when I say "erase," a lot of engineers secretly aren't erasing the take because they think that I'm going to come back in the room and maybe I'll want to grab something from a previous take. I'm already pretty confident about it and to me, it just creates this clutter. I just want the engineer to trust me that I'm going to be able to do it better. Listen to your singer. If she says "erase," just erase it—just let it go. I like things to be clean. I don't want to sort through a big old mess. And I don't want to fool myself into thinking I might have gotten it when my instinct is pretty correct in knowing if I didn't nail it yet.

You're always singing. You're always in a studio of some sort. I learned things from you back in the day when we were recording. That was like in the '90s. It was fun.

Yeah, that was a good time [*laughing*].

We're here as a service industry. We're not different than a barber, a waiter in a restaurant, or any other service industry. The way to get to the top is by giving good service to that person you're recording. When an artist or producer runs across a special engineer, they're going to try to keep that person in the camp—that's a good way to get job security, too. So many times, when I've asked my friends how they got started, they were recording vocals for a star and they did that really well. That sets up a psychological thing where if you do one thing well, you gain confidence that you can do the next thing well. Then everyone is liking your rough mix. The next thing you know, the rough mix is on the radio, and the next thing you know, you're Manny Marroquin! It's just that simple. Everything in our world has a person involved. And everything can either lead to something else or it can just as easily be the last day of your career. It's your choice.

8

Fixing Problems

by Bob Horn

When I was thinking about how to put this chapter together, I realized that my friend Bob Horn could probably do this better than me, so I want you guys to listen to Bob. He's really good at this, and you'll learn from him. Bob's going to take you through VocAlign and Melodyne, aligning and tuning vocals. To see more of Bob's great teaching, check out his streaming show called "Pro Studio Live" at www.prostudiolive.com. —D.P.

VOCALIGN AND MELODYNE

Using VocAlign

VocAlign, from Synchroarts, is an AudioSuite plug-in and it pretty much does exactly what the name says—it rhythmically aligns your vocal tracks. There are a couple tricks to VocAlign. Basically, you pick the one track you worked the hardest on and use it as your guide for the other tracks. Load the track with the rhythmic feel and vibe that you want into VocAlign by hitting "Capture." Select all tracks that need to be aligned to the guide track, then press the "Dub" button. Press the "Align" button to cause the selected Dub tracks to rhythmically conform to the captured guide track. Once all of the doubles have been aligned they will hopefully end up matching the rhythm of the guide track. Then the doubles will be nice and tight and they'll sound great together. I prefer to group them all and separate the phrases within the vocal section. I feel that VocAlign works a little better if you don't give it too much at once.

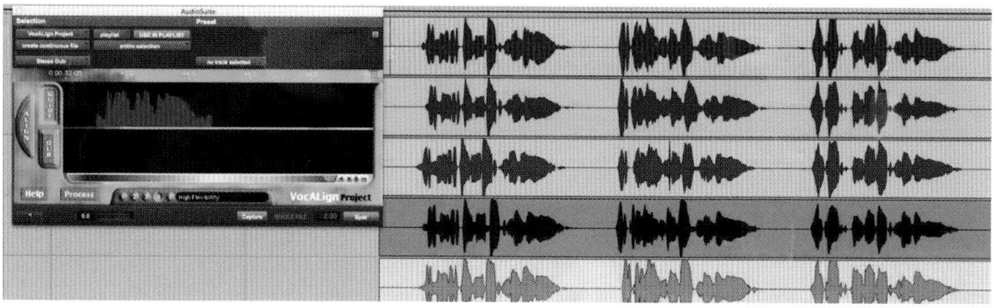

This is a hook on a song that I mixed a few months back. The vocals were actually perfect but I moved them around and made them rhythmically inaccurate, just for this example, so you could see what I frequently run up against. Some of these phrases are a little bit ahead of others, some are a little bit lagging, and if you zoom in on the waveforms, some of the notes are even different lengths. VocAlign will actually take all that and match the vocal phrases up perfectly.

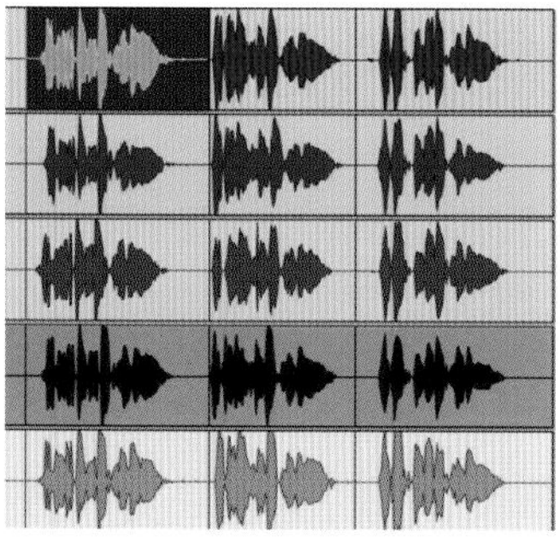

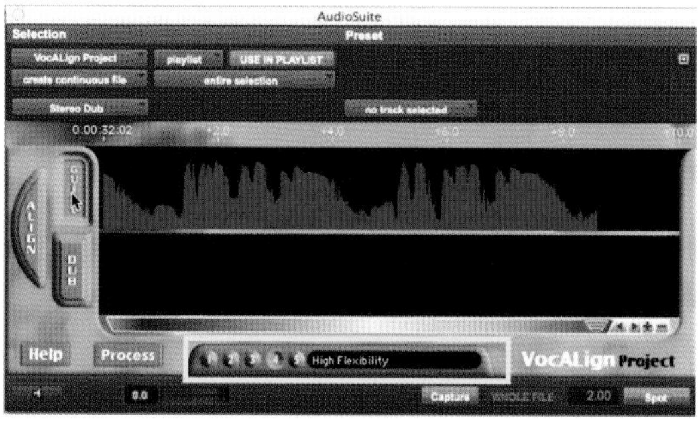

Here I divide the vocal tracks up into three separate phrases. We're going to use the first one, capture it, and then go to our double and capture that. So now, before I hit "align process," you'll notice below the window there is some flexibility in how perfectly VocAlign matches the guide track. You have flexibility here and I kind of like it on either 3 or 4. You can experiment with these. If you go to 1, it's super tight. If you go to 5, it's not quite as tight but it's still pretty tight. These settings let you get a double that's a little more natural or you can identically match the guide.

If there's any extra waveforms on a track—for instance if track 1 has a big breath but tracks 3 and 4 don't have those breaths—that breath can be perceived as part of the vocal waveform you're trying to align. When that happens, VocAlign sees the breath as an extra shape, or note, and can't accurately match everything up. So you want all of the waveforms to look about the same, even if they are not perfectly in time.

VocAlign magically transforms the doubled waveforms so they match that first one. It's just really a great tool to get your vocals to sound super tight. It makes the parts clean and tight and really increases the intelligibility of the lyrics.

Using Melodyne

In the last 15 years, our industry has gravitated towards perfectly tuned vocals in most genres. It's so common now that when you hear a vocal done naturally without tuning, it sounds off to some people, even if it's pretty well in tune. So for that reason alone, tuning is very important, just to sound modern. Some people say tuning is bad. Tuning is good! The effectiveness of tuning a vocal really has to do with the person doing the tuning and how good they are at their craft.

With subtle changes, vocals can be tuned so they sound very natural. You don't need much with a good singer. Obviously, there are extreme auto-tune effects. We're not talking about those. We're just talking about getting on pitch.

I prefer the Melodyne plug-in but there's also a standalone version. The plug-in is great because it's all within the DAW. You insert the Melodyne plug-in on the track you're working with and it just works. You don't have to export anything. It's great.

One thing that's important to know about Melodyne is that it actually records the track into the plug-in. It creates a new audio file on your hard drive, so you need to be conscious of where you insert the plug-in. You don't want to place Melodyne, for instance, after a compressor, because it's going to record the sound of that compressor. After you've recorded the vocal, when you go back for playback, nothing's going to happen when you adjust your compressor because it's no longer playing back the audio file. It's the track that was transferred to Melodyne playing back.

When I'm tuning vocals, I like to have a little bit of the music playing back at the same time. Some people get distracted by drums but if you just turn up the bass or grand piano, you'll have a solid reference to listen to so you're not just going by the lines when you're tuning. You can make better musical choices when you listen to the musical background. A lot of times I'll keep all of the tracks in but I'll turn the level down a bit so I can focus on the vocal tuning.

Controls

There are an array of tools available in Melodyne that let the user easily perform tasks that range from creating a synth-like T-Pain effect to simply minimizing pitch variations for a natural-sounding, musical, and emotional performance. Here I'll explain some of the Melodyne tools that I use most often.

Transfer Button. In Melodyne, hit the Track button, then hit play. Once the vocal track has been "transferred," it no longer plays back from this audio file. Instead, it plays back from the Melodyne plug-in. Therefore, it's very important that the Melodyne plug-in is inserted first in the DAW's plug-in insert chain. Any plug-in that is placed ahead of the Melodyne plug-in will be printed to the Melodyne track and will no longer affect the vocal track. In fact, the original vocal track can even be deleted and the track will still play back from its new Melodyne-generated audio file. If Melodyne is the first plug-in in the chain, all the plug-ins that follow will work as they normally would.

Transfer button

Blobs. The Melodyne display uses an X-Y axis. The X axis represents time and the Y axis represents pitch. Each waveform is represented by a red and orange blob on the screen. These waveforms are superimposed over the pitch and timing grid. The pitch of the vocal is represented by the vertical position of the waveform and the horizontal position represents timing. To make a note in-tune, move it to the correct pitch line.

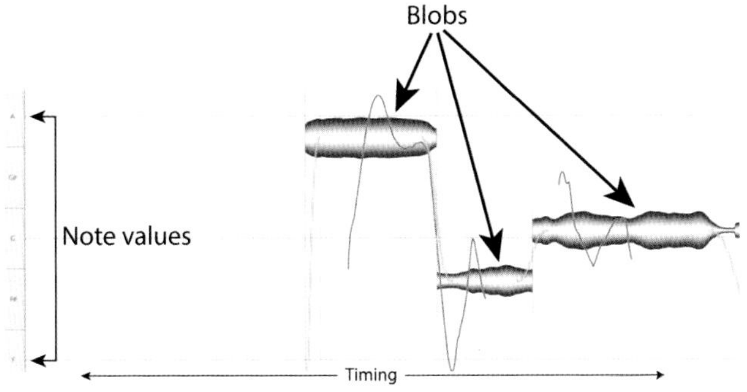

Blobs represent average pitch, timing, and amplitude. Drag a blob up or down to the note line of the correct pitch. Expand or contract the height of the blob to increase or decrease the volume.

Sizing the Window. The Melodyne window can be resized according to your preference. It is definitely easier to see the finer details when the window is larger. I always zoom in first so I can really see what I'm doing.

Main, Scroll, Zoom. It's easy to zoom in on the Melodyne window. If you click and hold on the tools, there are drop down tools, so with the Main Pointer Tool, you also can access the Scroll and the Zoom Tools.

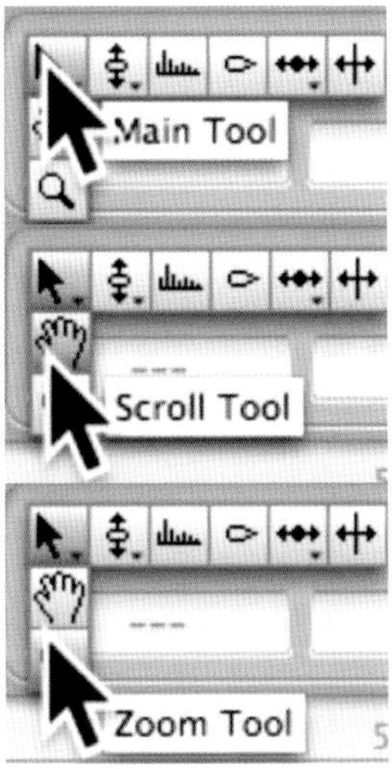

Main, Scroll, and Zoom Tools

Formant Tool. The Formant Tool can make something sound a little more masculine or feminine.

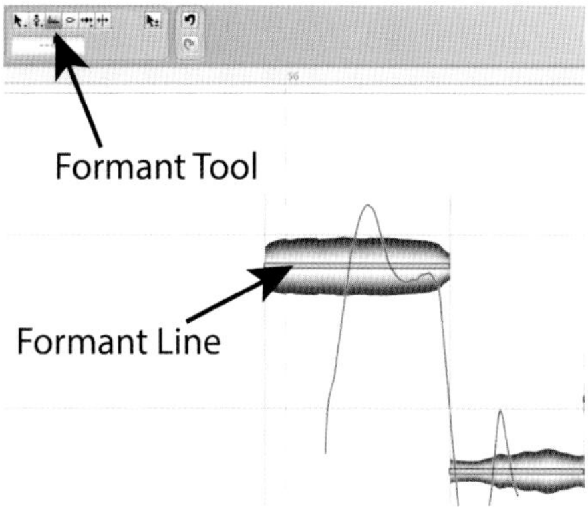

The Formant Tool adjusts the formant line that runs the length of the blob.

Volume Control. The volume of each segment can be adjusted by simply changing the height of the waveform by the Amplitude Tool. If a certain phrase jumps out because it's too loud or is hidden because it's too quiet, it's very helpful to adjust the level during the tuning process rather than relying on a compressor or volume automation later.

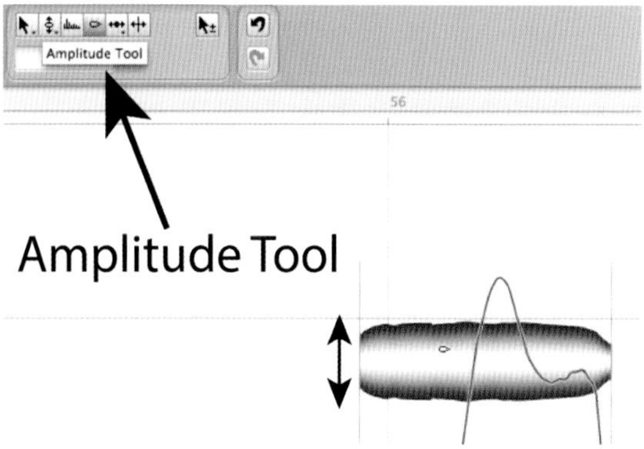

The Amplitude Tool expands or contracts the waveform height, increasing or decreasing the waveform volume.

Undo and Redo. As with every digital control, the Undo and Redo controls are very helpful.

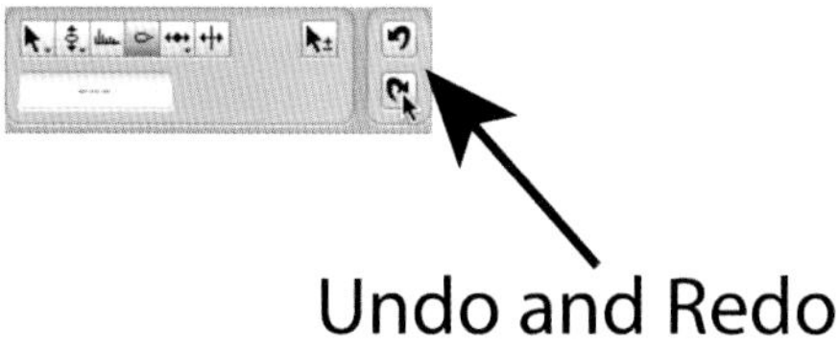

Undo and Redo

Time Stretching. If something's a little bit out of time, you can stretch it out or tighten it up. It's one of the most natural-sounding time waveform manipulators I've used. This tool is very helpful for getting notes on beat. If a vocalist has cut a note off early because he or she was out of breath, it's a simple matter to extend the note.

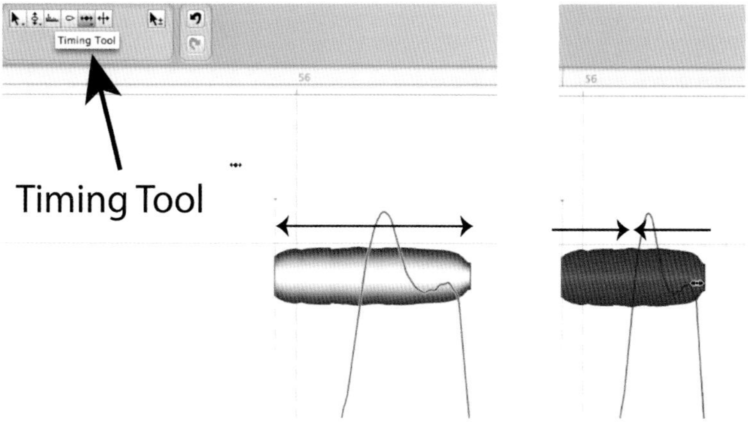

Time Stretching

Snap to Tuning Line. Once the vocal is tracked, a line displays the actual pitch of that tracked vocal. It displays pitch, vibrato, and the precise timing of all pitch changes. The red and yellow blob represents the waveform timing and amplitude but the line represents the pitch. It's very easy to see where the singer is sharp and flat and exactly how sharp or flat the track is. Many singers attack a note a little sharp and then they rest into that correct pitch after the attack. If you want, you can snap each vocal note to the exact pitch right away. It's more natural-sounding to leave some of the imperfections in place. Usually, a vocal track should sound like a vocalist performed it live but very well in tune.

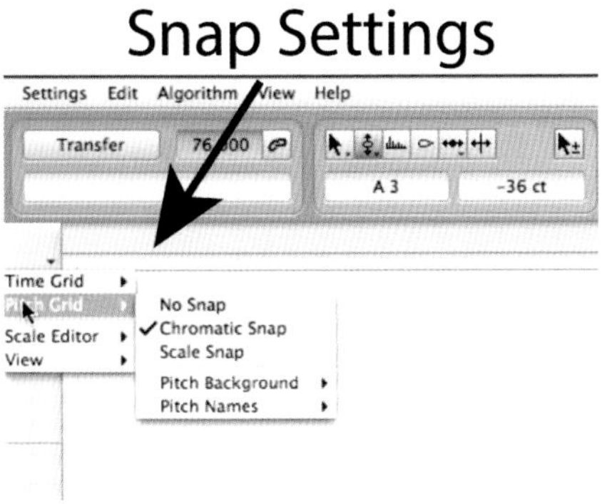

When moving blobs, you can choose to snap to chromatic pitches, to a scale, or manually without snapping.

Pitch Tool. The Pitch Tool drags the waveform blob sharp and flat, allowing the engineer to position it on the pitch line so that the note sounds in tune.

Pitch Tool

Pitch Modulation Tool. When the tuning line goes dramatically above and below the center pitch, such as when a singer has an overly exaggerated vibrato, the Pitch Modulation Tool is used to drag those over and under variations closer to the center line. At its extreme, this tool can flatten out the pitch line, which creates a synthesizer-like mechanical sound with no variation. However, the engineer can choose to decrease those variations by a little or a lot, which provides him or her the opportunity to partially tune the vocal, retaining the natural feel and emotion of the vocal performance, or to make the vocal notes unnaturally lock to a pitch grid like a piano or synthesizer.

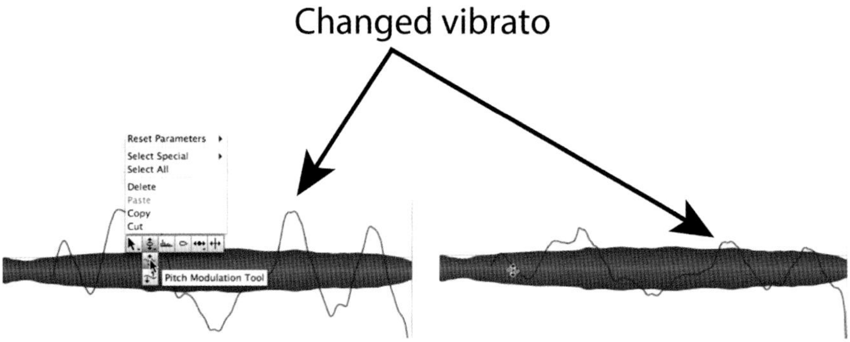

Notice the deep vibrato in left blob, varying from the F center pitch line down to E and up to F♯. This vocal spans three notes with a single sung note using vibrato. In the right blob, the Pitch Modulation Tool has reduced the modulation (variance in pitch), decreasing the amount of vibrato.

Note Separation Tool. Another important feature of Melodyne is the Note Separation Tool. Some waveforms contain runs that include multiple notes. This tool lets the user cut the waveform into separate notes so they can be tuned individually.

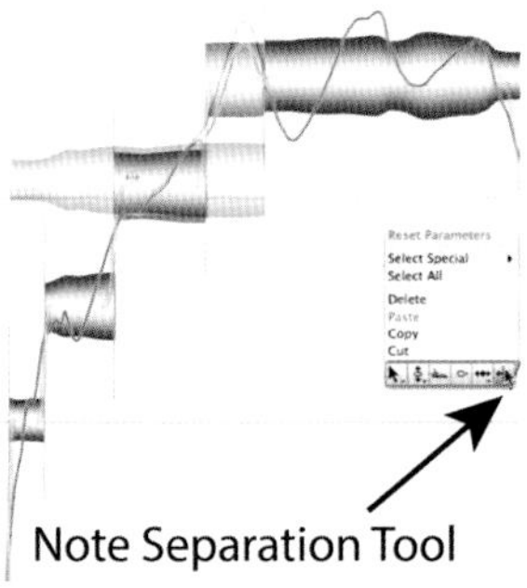

The original shaded waveform contains a three-note run that moves up to the main note but Melodyne only showed one waveform blob. The Note Separation Tool was used to cut the single waveform into individual notes so they could each be tuned separately.

Pitch Drift Tool. Another great Melodyne feature is the Pitch Drift Tool. The pitch of some notes go flat or sharp toward the end of the note. The Pitch Drift feature lets the engineer keep all of the vibrato and emotional inflections from the original take but it only fixes the sagging pitch at the end of the note. Whereas the Pitch Modulation Tool adjusts how much vibrato the singer uses, the Pitch Drift Tool keeps all the original amount of vibrato but it teeter-totters the tuning line over the length of the note. If the vocal starts to go sharp or flat at the end of the note, you can teeter the tuning line back and forth so the pitch centers on the note line.

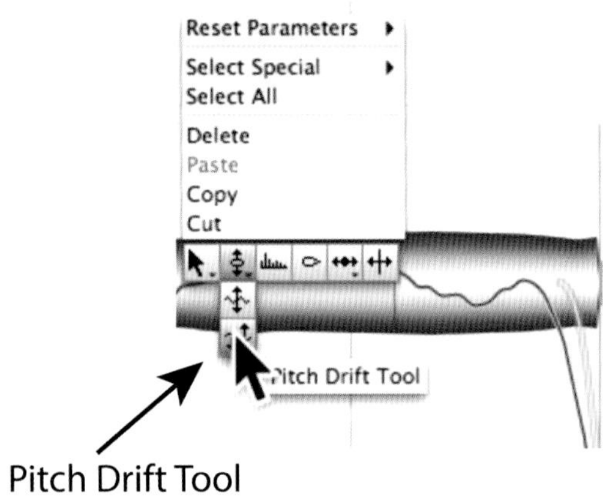

Pitch Drift Tool

Corner Adjustment Tool. Some singers tend to glide into every note. You don't want to completely get rid of that aspect of the performance because the results will sound very robotic. But you can use the Corner Adjustment Tool to control how much time those slides take. You can keep the energy and personality of the performance while still tightening up the note-to-note transitions.

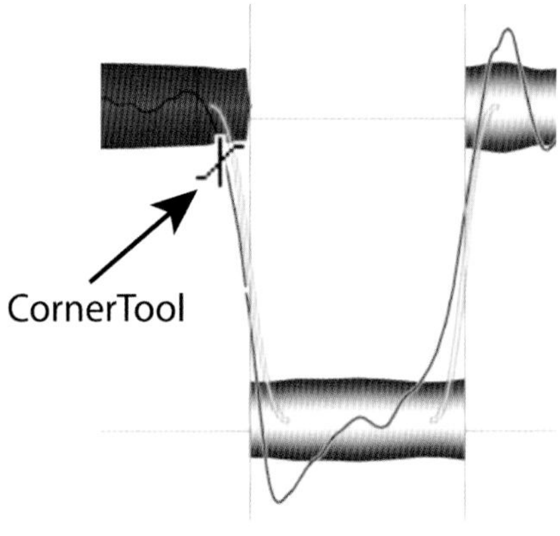

The Corner Adjustment Tool controls the speed of slides between notes.

Correct Pitch. If a singer has pretty accurate pitch and timing, Correct Pitch mode can be very helpful and extremely fast. Simply highlight all or part of the vocal track and press the Correct Pitch button in the upper right corner. However, if the singer is a little rougher, Correct Pitch mode might place some of the notes on the incorrect pitch. It's usually best to go through the vocal track manually to fine-tune each part of the track for the most natural-sounding musical performance.

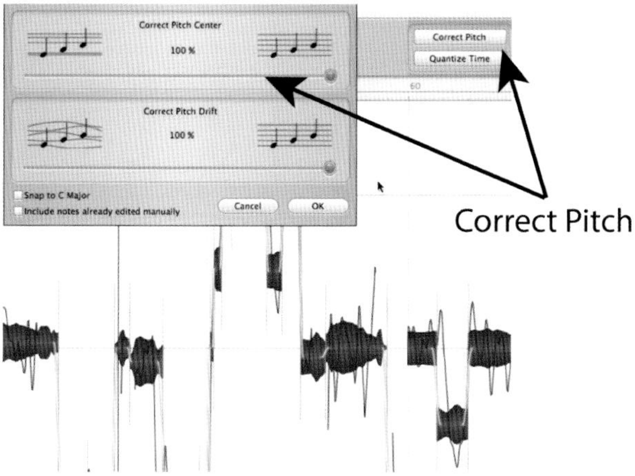

Correct Pitch button

When Melodyne is used as a plug-in rather than as a standalone, it is simple to make adjustments throughout the mixing process. Go through the track and make all the changes that are needed, then continue mixing. If a vocal flaw stands out later during mixdown, simply select Melodyne on the vocal track insert and pick up where you left off tuning the vocal.

9

Mixing Vocals

When I'm working on a vocal sound, I'm not trying things randomly. I'm really just trying to enhance what the singer gave us. We've got such great tools to work with! If you can't make a good record now, it's certainly not because there aren't enough mixing and recording tools available. Back in the day, we would take years to master one tool. Now we get a new tool every day! I'm having a little bit of difficulty finding the time to master every plug-in but I'm continuing to try. Master as many as you can. But always keep in mind that it's better to master 10 plug-ins than it is to just superficially know how to operate presets on 100 plug-ins.

There's an old saying, "Just fix it in the mix." Well I'm not a big believer in that, even though I earn a living as a mixer. It is best to get the tracks recorded perfectly, capturing the best performance possible from each singer and instrumentalist. But let's look at some ways we can make things better during the mix.

MIXING ESTHERO

On the vocal track that we recorded through the U 87, I heard a little bit too much somewhere between 400 and 600 Hz, so I backed off that range a bit. And I felt like it needed a little more top end, so I added a couple dB at 5 kHz, and I took out a couple dB at 2 kHz.

McDSP AE400 Active Equalizer. I used a McDSP AE400 multiband compressor on this vocal. I use this plug-in a lot on vocals and I think of it as an equalizer. Even though it is a 4-band compressor, the result is a change in the balance of those bands. On this vocal I'm using the AE400 to compress the band centered on 600 Hz; therefore, it turns down that band anytime the level exceeds the threshold.

McDSP AE400 Active Equalizer

UAD Massenburg High-Resolution EQ. I also like to use the UAD Massenburg High-Resolution EQ a lot on vocals. It handles the high frequencies above 10 kHz up to the Nyquist frequency of 20 kHz much more accurately than other plug-ins. On this vocal sound, I've cut 300 Hz by a little over 2 dB and I've set the high pass filter at 102 Hz with a 6 dB per octave slope.

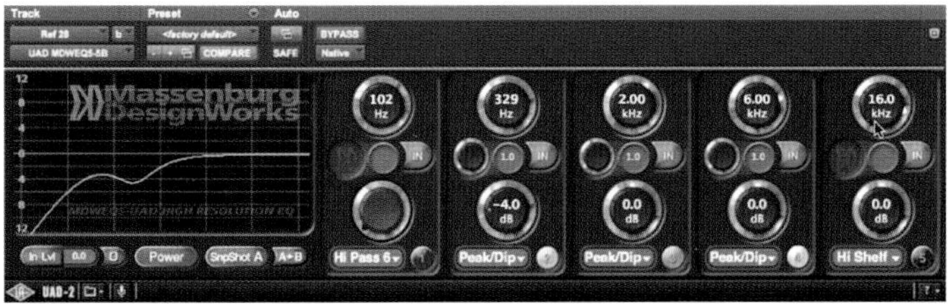

UAD Massenburg High-Resolution EQ

Tube-Tech CL 1B. For a compressor on this vocal track, I really like the Tube-Tech CL 1B. The attack and release settings are pretty standard and I prefer the 2:1 ratio setting for this track.

Softube Tube-Tech CL 1B

Waves MV2. The Waves MV2 combines a limiter and an expander in one plug-in, so it limits the loud parts a little and turns up the quiet parts a little. I'm just setting it for a series of very tiny changes.

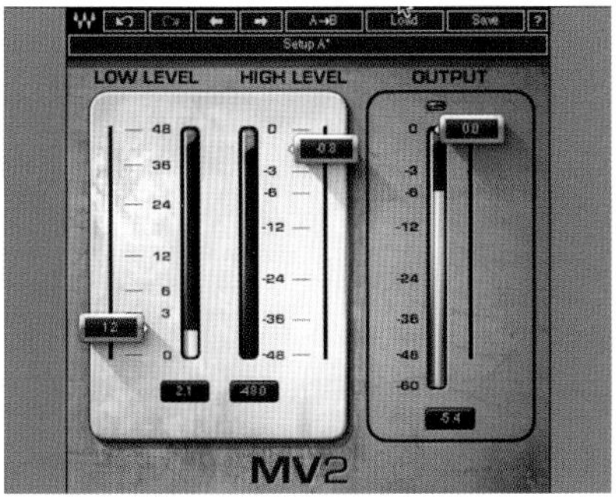

Waves MV2

Experimental Audio Bricasti Design M7 Control. There is a lot we could do with effects but I noticed that Esthero really liked the long EMT plate when Leandro recorded the vocal, so we'll start with that. And then I added a chamber from the Bricasti.

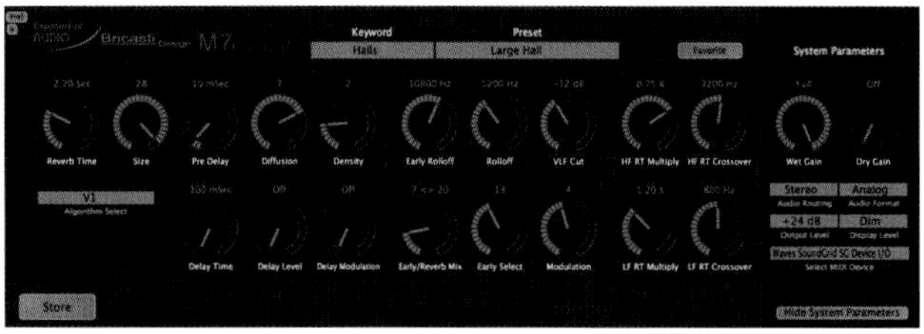

Experimental Audio Bricasti Design M7 Control

RMX 16 Digital Reverberation System. Here's a trick I learned from Alan Myerson. Try a non-linear reverb—any kind will work. I like the classic RMX 16 Digital Reverberation System, either the classic hardware or the UAD plug-in version. Even when I just insert it, it's like magic! Non-linear reverberation doesn't decay naturally like a concert hall or any other normal room. Instead it can swell up after a note, which tends to lengthen the sound. It's a great effect! I like to use it along with a multi-tap delay. Try it.

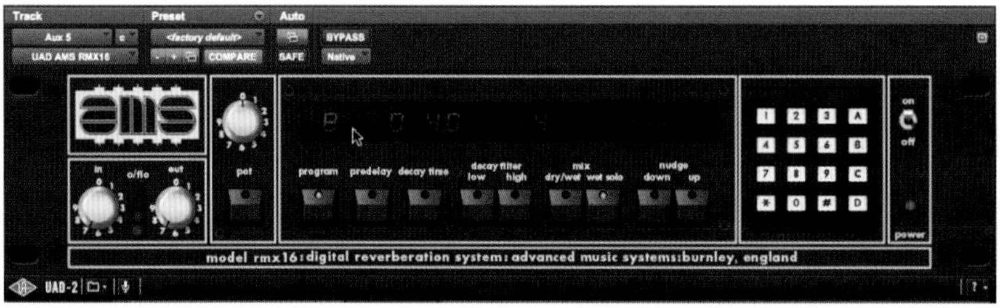

RMX 16 Digital Reverberation System

Clip Gain. I like to use Clip Gain to smooth out vocal sections and to enhance a performance. In Pro Tools, Clip Gain controls the size and volume of the audio wave. Clip Gain can either be adjusted globally to an entire clip or you can work with the

Clip Gain Line, which lets you draw in level changes in the same way as Volume Automation. So why not just use volume automation? It's because Volume Automation simply adjusts the volume at the end of your signal change, after all inserted plug-ins and/or hardware. I want to, instead, adjust the level of the waveform at the beginning of the signal chain so I can control how the vocal hits the compressors and everything else in the chain. If I can create just the right dynamics at the beginning of the chain, the compressors won't need to work as hard to control the level and the vocal sound will be much cleaner—it'll just sound better.

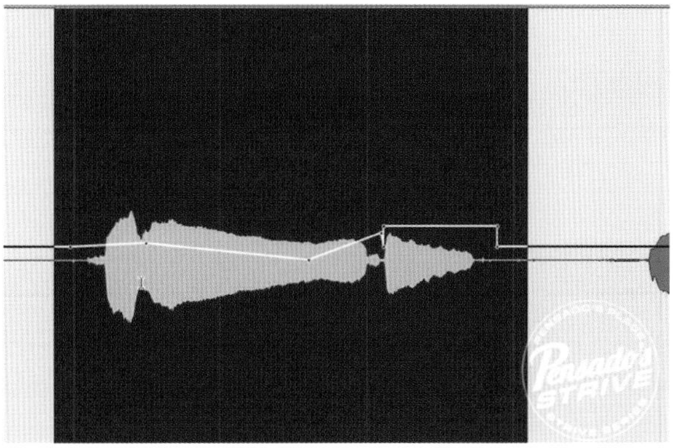

Pro Tools' Clip Gain Line view

BREAKING DOWN RAP VOCALS

When mixing any vocal, including a rap vocal, you don't have to EQ it and get it sounding perfect before you start working on the music and the beat. A lot of times, especially when I'm working on a rap or hip-hop song, I like to start with the beat. I like to bring the vocal in every now and then to see where it's sitting so I can make sure I leave a spot for it in the final product. Quincy Jones likes to say, "You should always leave a little space in the recording studio for God to walk in." I think you should also leave a little space in the mix so the vocal can sit right, whether it's a rap or not. With some forms of music, like hip-hop, there's not always as much dynamic in the tracks as you might want. A great way to get those dynamics is through the rap vocal's timing, feel, and energy. Engineers sometimes tend to over compress, which destroys dynamics, energy, and excitement of the performance. Avoid using too much compression.

Compression

I like to use a lot of compressors but not have any one of them doing a lot. I like to just use each compressor for what it does best. I'd rather have a lot of little tiny bites taken out of the dynamics than have one big gesture, because that one gesture is going to effect the timing, the length of the words, and it has the potential of causing a lot of negative things to happen to the performance.

Here's an example of the processors I used in the vocal signal chain on a mix of "Twisted & Laidback" for Mike Rebel.

fabfilter Pro•Q2. There's nothing earth shattering happening with this EQ. The track just needed a little cleanup at a couple spots surrounding 500 Hz. I took 400 and 600 Hz down just a little bit, which helps emphasize the range between about 1 and 3 kHz.

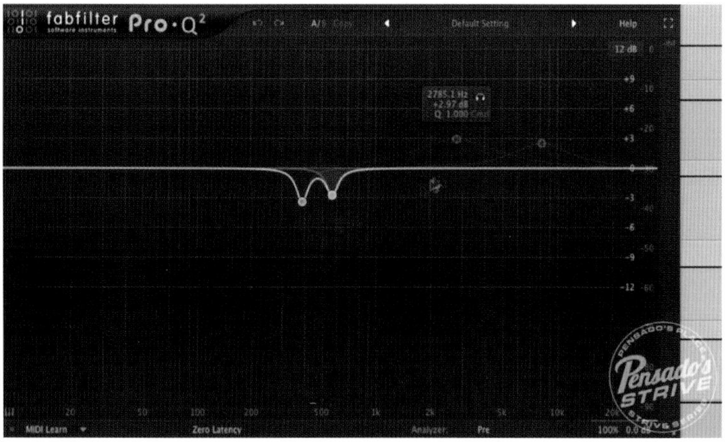

fabfilter Pro•Q2

UAD Massenburg DesignWorks MDEQ5 High-Resolution EQ. Again, I really like the MDW for what it does with the high frequencies. In this case, I have a high-frequency shelf boosted by a couple dB at 10 kHz. This EQ does a great job handling these upper frequencies. I've also used it to clean up some of the mid and low frequencies.

UAD Massenburg DesignWorks MDEQ5 High-Resolution EQ

Waves C4 Multiband Parametric Processor. I'm using the Waves C4 for compression and equalization. It's a 4-band compressor; however, by changing the relative balances between the frequency bands, it is constantly equalizing the signal depending on which frequencies are being compressed and by how much. I'm not hitting it very hard but it is giving us a little more clarity. If we use each tool for its strength, we can increase the perception of dynamics, even though we're actually taking some out. It's kind of a cool thing.

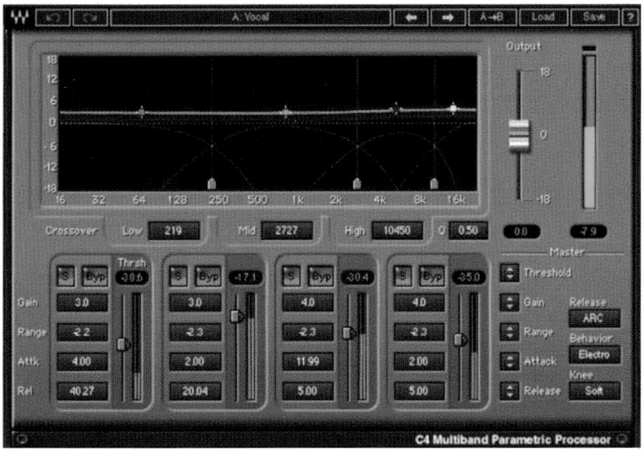

Waves C4 Multiband Parametric Processor

Waves MV2. I use the Waves MV2 a lot. One side helps you deal with some of the lower elements of the performance by turning them up. The other side is a simple limiter, so it helps control the louder elements of the performance. The MV2 is a big contributor to the sound and feel of the vocal performance. It helps shape the energy of the track and can even make certain words sound longer, because you can hear where they end better. Timing is not all about where a word starts. A lot of times where the word stops is actually more important than where it starts.

Waves MV2

McDSP AE400 Active Equalizer. I used the AE400 as an upward expander but only at 1 kHz. Expanding that frequency gave me the tempo and feel that I wanted. Highlighting that band at 1K really brought out "Alabama" and "Where my grandma from." "Grandma" is one of the most important words in the entire song.

McDSP AE400 Active Equalizer

Waves Renaissance Axx. The Axx is a plug-in that was made for guitar. Now you might say, "Dave, why you using a guitar plug-in on a vocal?" It is really a pretty simple compressor but it does a great job of accentuating the attacks of notes and words. In Rap music, the words are very important and they're particularly important in this song. Mike is telling the story about his childhood and he's making a lot of political points by doing that. I felt if I could enhance the consonants in a musical way, it would help reinforce the timing. He has great timing and I wanted the consonants to carry a lot of the rhythmic weight.

Waves Renaissance Axx

Waves CLA-76 Classic Compressor and L1 Limiter. I often use parallel compression on the vocal. On Mike's rap, I used an L1 with a CLA-76 and just squeezed the snot out of the parallel chain. Remember, this is a parallel chain, so the regular vocal track is still there along with all of the adjustments in EQ and compressors. That way we keep the dynamics from the original performance but we can tuck the parallel chain up underneath. That helps keep the vocal in your face and it provides more bottom-end warmth.

Waves L1 Limiter

Waves CLA-76 Classic Compressor

I wouldn't consider anything I did on Mike's vocal to be a difficult or high-level technique. I just heard and felt a need to help highlight the emotion in his performance. It's there but it just needs to be brought out in the mix. Sometimes the recording process can rob a little from the musical performance. Maybe something happens at the mic capsule or in the microphone electronics. Maybe the preamp wasn't just right. Each time the vocal goes through another electronic process, something's gained or something's lost. Each little change we made helped bring back the performance so that it works very well in the mix.

Applying Concepts

All of the concepts we just covered can be applied to virtually any style of music, whether rap, rock, hip-hop, country, blues, or pretty much anything else. They can also apply to some acoustic instrument performances. It's all about analyzing where the energy is and then constructing a signal chain that enhances that energy.

If these things don't come to you immediately then you're no different than me. It took me a long time to understand what I was trying to do with the vocal. I always just tried to make it sound good. I always put reverb on it because I thought you were supposed to. And if I could get something like a plate, I thought, okay, it needs a plate. I thought I should put a compressor on it but I didn't really know why.

I used a lot of different plug-ins. You don't necessarily need to use everything I did. If you don't have these exact plug-ins, just use the ones you have. This is a lot easier with fewer variables. The difference between you and me is not that I have better taste than you. The difference is simply that I can do what I do quicker. A pro works quicker, whereas an amateur works slower, but we should be doing the same exact things. Don't assume that just because you're not earning a living doing this, that you can't do it. You've got the taste. Nobody can take that away from you, because you've had that all your life.

Don't always try to get it perfect with just one piece of outboard gear or with just one plug-in. Take little chunks off—little bites—until you find the sound you're looking for.

10

Wrapping Up

In this section, we're going to talk about de-essing, dividing the vocal track into sections, Mid-Side EQ, and, comping vocals.

DE-ESSING

There's a lot of performance energy and vibe in the sibilant "s" sounds. One of my dear friends and a truly great producer, Ron Fair, won't let me use a de-esser. He points out that there's too much energy and vibe and emotion that could potentially be damaged in the de-essing process.

Sometimes a de-esser is a valuable tool. I like to use two de-essers. One is kind of gentle and the other one grabs it. One of my favorite de-essers is the fabfilter Pro•DS because it really helps you isolate things so you can hear and adjust what you want to take out. I like to use it as a gentle de-esser. Once that is set, I'll insert another de-esser and set it for extreme de-essing but with a high threshold so it isn't making dramatic changes. I like the Massey De:Esser because it provides a lot of control too. I can set it so it backs up the fabfilter Pro•DS and won't let anything get too out of control.

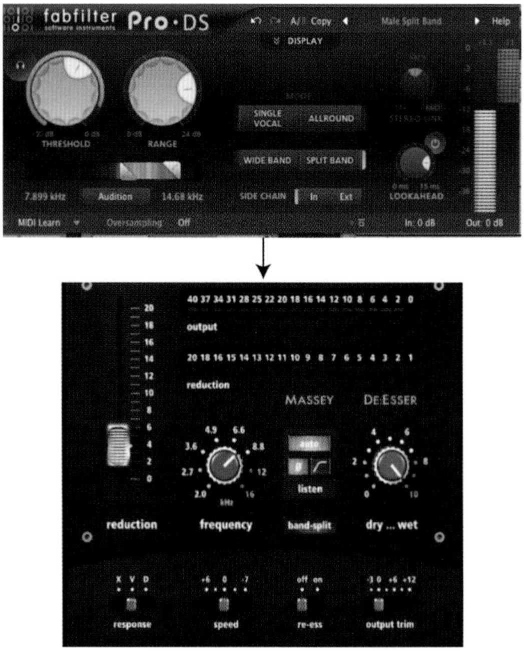

I like to use the fabfilter Pro•DS to gently de-ess, then after that, in the insert chain, I like the Massey De:Esser to make sure nothing gets too out of control.

Sometimes I'll just use volume automation and be very specific about which parts of the words I adjust. This isn't like using de-essers, because it turns down the entire level and not just a narrow frequency band; but you can still get great results and it can be a good option. Once the volume automation is set, I might still put a gentle de-esser in the signal path. Each case is different.

You might say, "Dave, why don't you just EQ the sibilance out?" But that's a whole different sound. Sometimes the frequencies that are the biggest problem for the "s" sounds are the frequencies that give life to the other sounds. Trying to fix the vocal esses by finding the right EQ is like going butterfly hunting with a bazooka. It's just not efficient and it's going to needlessly mess something up.

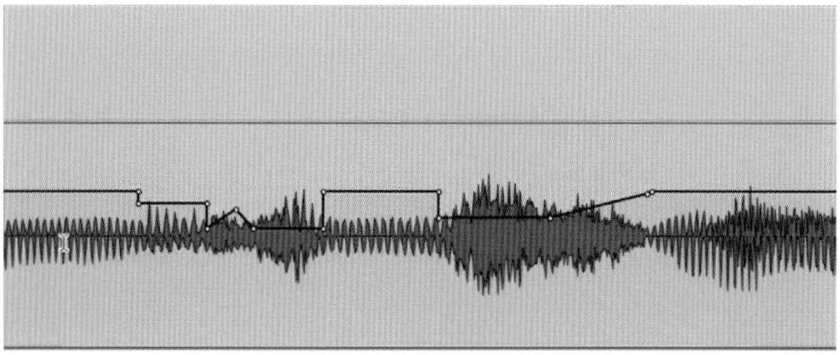

Notice that I've been very specific about setting the volume automation to help minimize problematic esses.

You can usually find a combination of things do a good job of controlling esses but the main consideration is that you keep the energy going. I hear songs all the time that are overly de-essed, and it can really decrease the amount of energy in the performance, so be careful. Also, when you're in the studio, the esses always sound louder than when you leave. When Ron Fair would tell me to just leave them alone, I'd go, "Man, those are so loud." And then I'd hear the song on the radio and the esses would sound just right. When you focus on them while you're mixing, it gets to the point where all you hear are the esses. You need to train your ear and your brain not to focus on them. If you work on a mix and you're fighting to get the de-essers set right, try not to let it leave the studio until you hear it with fresh ears the next day.

DIVIDING THE VOCAL TRACK INTO SECTIONS

There are so many things going on in a vocal track. It's not like a kick drum or a snare drum, which will be roughly the same at the beginning of the song as it is at the end. The kick drum EQs that you start with can probably work well for at least 85% of the song, but vocals aren't like that. They change from whispery and soft to full-on Christina Aguilera volume and power. Some singers get a little more 1.5–2K in their voice as they increase in volume, which is a good thing because it makes you feel like they're singing louder.

Vocals are very dynamic and you frequently need to automate each section of the song differently. You can't just have a static EQ or compression. You might want to automate multiple compression parameters and you should definitely consider automating EQ. Sometimes I'll divide the lead vocal up into three basic sections—I'll take that one track and create three tracks out of it. I'll put the soft parts in one track, the regular parts in another track, and my loud vocal effects sounds in the third track. So don't be afraid to take advantage of what the digital world has to offer. In the analog world when I mixed Christina—before digital—I used to have her vocals spread out over eight faders and each fader had a different sound. I would mix it like a keyboard. I had everything memorized with my eight fingers and I'd pull these two faders up, or this fader up, or this one, or that one, in combination of the two, depending on how she was singing. It's so much easier today. Copying each type of performance to its own track doesn't degrade the quality, it's fast and easy, and it lets you tackle each section with the best tools for each different vocal sound.

MID-SIDE EQ

I'm a sucker for harmonies—I love, love, love harmonies. There are a lot of different ways to mix the background vocals. For example, let's say I've got a four-part harmony with four tracks of each part. I'll experiment by trying to put the lower notes toward the middle, and the higher notes toward the outside of the mix. I never get too close to the middle, because that's where we're going to place the lead vocal. And then I try to arrange the parts so it sounds like a chord to me—like a piano. Sometimes on a piano you hear four notes like they're just one thing—that's the impression I like to get with the harmonies. I like to get the balance so perfect that everything blends together without having one note standing out above the others.

Dynamics are your friend, though. It's okay for things to kind of pop out here or there—that's what we call "music." I like to do something a lot of people don't think about; I use a technique called MS, which stands for Middle and Side, or Mid-Side. It's an old stereo mic technique. When I first started engineering, I thought I invented the MS technique. One day I went to the studio and I told my boss, "Hey man, I invented this new thing." And he said, "Well Dave, that's kinda cool but you didn't invent that. That's been around since the '40s." So there you go. But this technique is basically a stereo mic technique I've modified in the digital domain to apply to the vocal tracks instead of applying it to the microphones. When setting up the MS microphone technique, you use a cardioid mic pointing at the source along with a figure-eight pointing to the sides (90 degrees off-axis to the source). The figure-eight mic is sent to two separate tracks that are hard-panned apart. Then you invert the phase on one of the figure-eight sides and it gives you a very nice stereo width—it's a really cool thing. This technique collapses to mono very well, because once it's in mono, the two side mics cancel out because they're 180 degrees out-of-phase. That leaves you with the sound of one single cardioid mic.

Waves CENTER Plug-In. There's an easy way to get an effect that's a lot like the sound of MS EQ. The Waves plug-in called CENTER is not an MS plug-in but it provides a similar effect and what it does can be, in some ways, even cooler than the MS technique. CENTER has two main faders: one to control the center image volume and one to control the volume of the sides. Once you have the background vocals mixed, you can insert the CENTER plug-in and clear out room in the center of the mix for the lead vocal by moving the backgrounds to the sides. It's a great effect. When you move the background vocals out to the sides a bit, it sounds like you've turned the lead vocal up even though the you haven't. Moving the backgrounds to the sides unmasks the lead vocal track—it removes the competition from the middle—so the lead can be heard better.

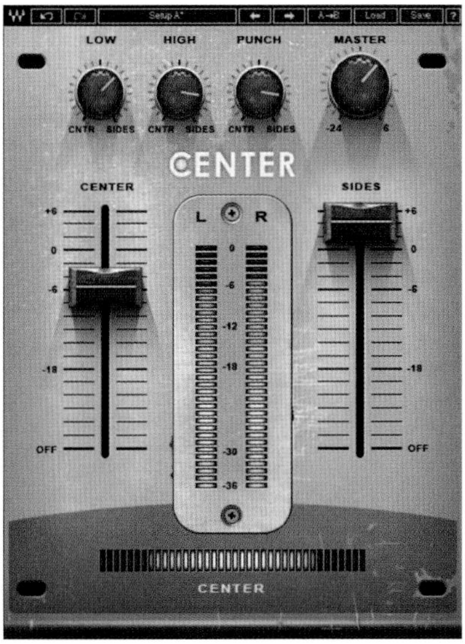

Waves CENTER

McDSP Filter Bank F202. Once the background vocals are moved out to the sides, you'll be able to hear them better. Sometimes that means the high frequencies might seem louder. When that happens, it's a good idea to run them through a plug-in like the McDSP FilterBank F202. Using the variable high pass filter to trim just the right amount of highs helps the backgrounds blend into the mix better so they don't compete with the lead vocal.

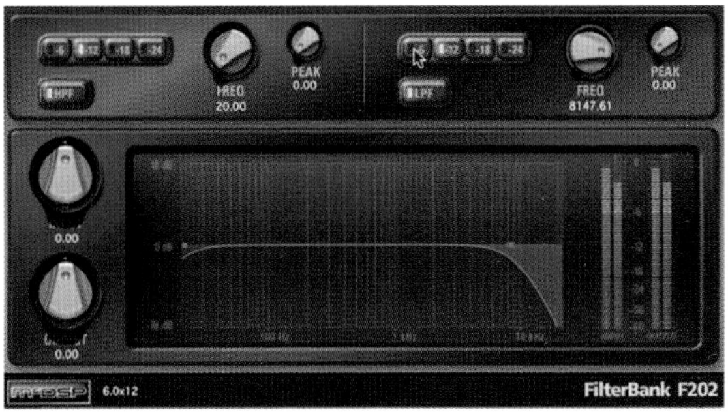

McDSP FilterBank F202

fabfilter Pro•Q2. The fabfilter Pro•Q2 is one of my favorites plug-ins. In addition to having a multiband Mid-Side mode, the mid and side images can be equalized separately. This is a great-sounding plug-in and you can tune the sound so the background vocal sits in just the right place and stays out of the way of the lead vocal. This technique also works for guitars or even for drums.

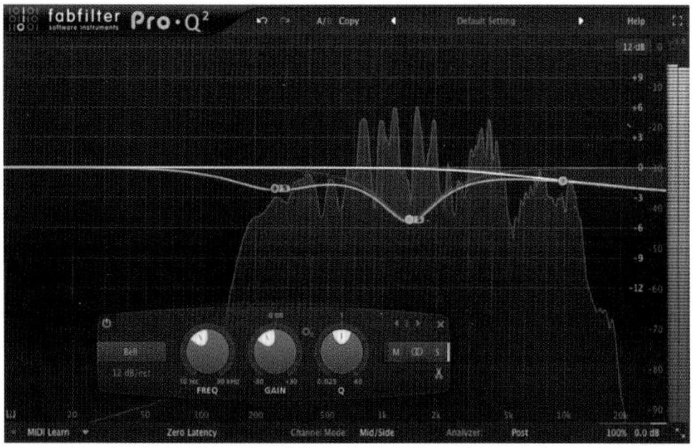

The M and S buttons to the right of the Q control on the fabfilter Pro•Q2 let you select which of the two components are being equalized.

AUXES

I typically use five or six auxes as subgroups in my mixes. I send tracks to the auxes and then feed the auxes back into the main mix. When the mix is divided into groups like this, there is great flexibility as the mix comes together. It makes it easy to customize the group levels and effects for each musical section if that's called for. When I'm mixing, I'm likely to route the following musical groups through stereo auxes and back into the main mix bus:

Vocals. I use one or two vocal auxes frequently with the background vocals on their own aux. I also set up an aux for the lead vocal.

Drums. I set up a drum aux so I can take my drums and dial them back in the verse a little, then I'll kick them up in the chorus. As the song progresses, I might make the drums a little louder on each chorus and sometimes I'll add a little more mid-range to the drums in the choruses to make them feel a little louder. It's all about creating a musical flow.

Music. I set up a music aux that contains everything except the vocals. The music aux is great. It's frightening how many times you'll think the mix is just perfect and you'll wonder if maybe the music level should be lowered, and when you lower it, the mix just comes alive. Or maybe it's the other way around and the mix comes alive when you raise the music level. It's hard to do that without having all of the music (drums, bass, guitars, keys, etc.) there on one aux.

Bass guitar. I'll put the bass on an aux if I'm working on a rock track.

Guitars. A lot of times I'll put all the guitars on an aux.

Effects. I put the effects returns on an aux. I like to solo just the outputs of the effects. Sometimes that lets me hear if the middle is too full. If it is, I like to use the MS EQ trick for the entire effects group. The Matthew Lane DrMS Spatial Processor is one of my favorite MS plug-ins. It has a lot of damn knobs and I'm not sure what a lot of these on the bottom even do but my buddy Matthew Lane does. We've put together some great presets that my other buddy, Dylan Dresdo, came up with. Very quickly, you can clear out as much of the middle image as you need, leaving the perfect space for the lead vocal.

Matthew Lane DrMS Spatial Processor

COMPING

Every vocal producer develops a method for working with the lead vocalist. He or she needs to find a natural workflow that gets the best performance out of the singer. My strength is that I can help the singer deliver a great emotional performance. I prefer to make decisions while we're tracking—sometimes you have to make decisions from the beginning. My goal is to have just one track of vocals—maybe two—and I try to punch in to repair anything that needs to be re-sung.

I like to record the singer from top to bottom. We might practice it a couple of times, which I prefer to do on a day other than the official tracking date so the singer isn't getting worn out before he or she really starts to get the music. If all the vocals are done in one day, I want to make sure I'm capturing that person at the peak of their excitement, which tends to be during takes one, two, or three. If you've had to spend time getting the tune down, take a break to let the singer regroup but don't rest too long or the singer's voice will change. When you come back, record two or three passes and try to keep the flow going. Try not to lose your momentum. Then pick the best take and work from there. Find the parts you don't like and punch in to replace them.

Another way to record vocals, which is probably used more often than the method I prefer, involves recording anywhere from 4 to 20 or 30 takes and then compiling (comping) the best parts of each take into the master lead vocal track.

Some producers like to record three or four complete takes and then they'll start working on each section of the song, recording multiple takes of verse one until they think they have the right material to comp together. Then they'll record several takes of verse two until they think they have enough material to comp together a great second verse; and they'll continue like that through the entire song. Sometimes the takes will be recorded on the same day and sometimes they'll be recorded on different days. Once they have everything recorded, they'll go through the takes and choose the very best parts to put on the master vocal track. Pro Tools provides a great way to comp vocals. Logic is great at it too.

There are a lot of ways to comp vocals. What's best for me might not be best for you. You need to spend some time and develop your own technique that works best for you. Comping is very useful for vocals but it also works very well on guitar and bass tracks and it can even work very well for drum parts.

Above all, the takes and portions of takes you select for the comped track need to be musical, which doesn't necessarily mean they have to be perfect. Sometimes the imperfections add emotion and musical power. Many of the recordings we fall in love with have imperfections. When you strive too hard for perfection, you're often destroying energy, performance, and uniqueness. It can be the imperfections in music that make it fun to listen to. If you don't believe me, listen to some of your favorite records and you'll hear they're not perfect. The great singers never worried about perfection and pitch as much as they worried about performance and energy. Listen to Whitney Houston, Mariah Carey, Gladys Knight, and Aretha Franklin. Those singers didn't try to hit notes, they just sang the song. That's something to be aware of when you're recording a vocalist. Go for the performance. If something gets a little out, we've got plenty of tools available to fix most any problem.

Conclusion

I want to leave you with some important parting thoughts. When one of my heroes told me he did something this way or she did something that way, I just blindly followed. That stymied my growth as an engineer. You would think having access to that information would have sped up my growth but it didn't. Bob Clearmountain, one of my heroes, told me that he took 300 or 400 Hz out of a kick drum. Man, for about two years I ruined every kick drum I got ahold of except for maybe one or two where that particular technique actually worked. Bob really meant that he takes something out in that region from 200–500 Hz. But I was just blindly doing what he literally said, whether it needed it or not. With that in mind, please pay close attention to the problem I'm trying to solve or a technique I'm trying to implement and realize that I'm working hard to shape a specific song. Everything might be different on the next song because it requires a different approach. As engineers, it's our job to shape a mix so that the song communicates its message to the listener.

There's no one-size-fits-all when it comes to recording and mixing techniques. I can't tell you the number of times, early in my career, I discovered what I thought was a really great vocal sound and thought I had the answer. I'd be thinking, "Man, I'm gonna change music!" Then the next singer would come in and I wouldn't change a thing—not the mic, the placement, preamp, the gobos—nothing! However, with a new singer on a different day, the sound wasn't good at all. In fact, it sounded pretty horrible. So as you're learning, assimilating knowledge, and filtering all that knowledge through who you are, don't get too locked into what other people do. Rather, use what they say to help find your own ways to record. If you want to be competitive in the marketplace, you need to compete with your techniques, your sounds, with your skillset, and with your taste. That's what gives you value in the world. Don't be a copy of anybody. Take a little longer, get the skills you need to do the work, read books, scour the internet, and then take all the techniques you come across and figure out why they work, and more importantly, figure out how they can work for you. Use your own musical taste to guide the way you apply different technique to each musical situation. I'll see you on the charts real soon.

About the Author

Dave Pensado is one of the recording industry's preeminent mix engineers. With multiple Grammy nominations and wins under his belt, he has had an astounding career. Christina Aguilera, Pink, Shakira, Beyoncé, Flo Rida, Afrojack, and Frank Ocean are a fraction of the superstars who keep him on speed dial. From pop to hip hop, country to Latin, and R&B to alternative, Pensado's special niche is making radio-friendly records while enhancing artistic intent.

In 2010, Dave Pensado and his manager started a web series entitled *Pensado's Place*. The show is wildly popular, is seen in over 150 countries by 600,000 people a month, and is used as curriculum in over 100 colleges around the globe. Every week audio artisans who work with superstars like Coldplay, Kanye West, Rascal Flatts, and more join Pensado to discuss all things audio. The show has been featured in *Forbes, Huffington Post, Boston Globe, and Last Call with Carson Daly* among others.

With all the success, what is his favorite part of his career? "Nothing is better than being able to teach," says Pensado. "The ability to share and watch it positively impact a life is incredibly powerful." It's that ethos that makes Dave Pensado so revered by his peers and makes him a legend to his fans.